The Dysfunctional Dance Of The Empath And Narcissist

CREATE HEALTHY RELATIONSHIPS
BY HEALING CHILDHOOD TRAUMA

Rita Louise, PhD

Copyright © 2020 by Rita Louise, PhD

No part of this book may be reproduced or utilized in any form or by any means: electronic, mechanical or otherwise, including photocopying, recording or by any informational storage and retrieval system without permission in writing from the author.

Although the author has researched all sources to ensure the accuracy and completeness of the information contained within this book, no responsibility is assumed for errors, inaccuracies, omissions, or inconsistency herein. Any slights of people, places or organizations are completely and totally unintentional.

ISBN # 978-0-9758649-5-1

Library of Congress Control Number: 2019919108

First Edition

Printed Dallas, TX, USA

This book is dedicated to all of the men and women who have survived a life filled with trauma and abuse.

Happiness is possible.

Acknowledgements

I would like to take a moment to thank all of the beautiful people who have helped me in my journey from dysfunction to living a blessed life.

First and foremost, to Dr. Fran Assaf, DC, who held my hand as I went through the dark night of the soul. Dr. Fran, I would have never made it through without you.

To Debbie Adams Gullett who let me borrow her brain and bounce things off of it. Deb, I didn't mean to make you cry when you read this text, but I hope it helped you on your own journey.

Thanks also go to Chris Rice, LPC, who helped me to understand what a healthy relationship is like versus one filled with abuse. Who knew?

And last, but never least, to Lieutenant Colonel Barney Patrick Morris (US Army Retired) for just loving me. Thank you!

Contents

Introduction 1
My Story 1
The Many Shades Of Abuse 19
    Physiological Impact Of Abuse 21
    Was I Abused? 26
    Parenting Styles 30
    Inside A Parent's Mind: What Were They Thinking? 34
    Inside The Abused Mind 37
        Early Attachment Patterns 38
        Core Or Limiting Beliefs 45
        Defense / Coping Mechanisms 57
    Family Roles 65
Beyond The Physical Body 71
    The Aura And Subtle Bodies 73
    The Chakras 76
    How It All Works: Energy Flow and the Subtle Energy System 81
    The Energy Of Thoughts & Emotions 84
In The Moment 88
    Emotional Triggers 90
    The Present Moment 93

- Intrusive Thoughts ... 94
- The Empath & Narcissist ... 103
  - The Creation Of Empaths And Narcissists ... 108
  - The Anatomy Of An Empath ... 113
    - Highly Sensitive People ... 115
    - Empaths ... 117
    - People Pleasing: The Aversion To Displeasing ... 121
  - The Anatomy Of A Narcissist ... 126
    - The Covert Narcissist ... 131
    - Behind The Mask Of The False Self ... 133
    - What Is Narcissistic Entitlement Really? ... 134
- The Dysfunctional Dance Of The Empath And Narcissist ... 138
  - The Lifecycle Of A Narcissistic Relationship ... 143
    - The Narcissistic Relationship - Part 1 ... 144
    - The Narcissistic Relationship - Part 2 ... 147
    - The Narcissistic Relationship - Part 3 ... 154
- The Thrill Is Gone ... 158
  - The Addiction Of Trauma Bonds ... 162
  - Narcissistic Withdrawal ... 164
  - Exit Strategy ... 167
  - Rising From The Ashes ... 171
- The Journey To Me-dom ... 177
  - Starting Over ... 182

Addressing The Fear Of Change 185
Will The Real Me Please Stand Up? 188
The Four Selves 190
Mindfulness 211
Mindfulness Practice 216
Journaling For Health And Well Being 225
Letting Go And Letting God 229
Addressing Anger And Resentment 230
Forgiving Yourself 233
I Was Such A Fool 234
Steps To Forgiveness 236
Develop An Attitude Of Gratitude 238
Energy Medicine 242
Ritual Purification 246
Grounding 253
Interacting With Your Aura 258
Aura Fluffing 259
Deprogramming 263
Healing With Flower Power 267
Cutting The Cords That Bind Us 271
Moving On 279
Working With The Law Of Attraction 283
Internet What? 290

Then What... 295
Boundaries: The Foul 10 Letter Word 298
Before I Go 301

Introduction

If you have experienced a pattern of toxic relationships plaguing your life, you probably do not understand why you keep getting into these hurtful situations in the first place. People do not go looking for the rotten apple at the bottom of the barrel, yet for some reason, we repeatedly bring them into our lives.

I know that was not my goal. Over the years, I finally accepted the fact that it was my lot in life, that I would always attract awful men. I was a failure at relationships. I would continually hope that the next man in my life would be better and treat me kinder. But, relationship success alluded me. That is until a chain of events shifted my perspective on my relationships and myself. This set me on a journey of healing that I will share with you. So, if the idea of learning to love yourself and by extension, finding someone who will honestly love you back is what you seek, then your dreams can come true. I know. It happened to me.

My Story

I feel it is essential to start this journey, our journey, with a brief discussion of my achievements. It is not because I want to let everyone know how great I am, but instead for you, the reader, to see how, on the outside, I seemed to have my life together. Honestly, I thought I did. This misconception continued until a series of events transpired that shattered the illusion. My psyche entered into the dark night of the soul. With it was the hope of a new life, a whole new me emerging on the other side.

The change, or should I say revelation, was dramatic and without ceremony. It was put right-square in front of my face, and I had no choice but to deal with it. So, I am going to start with who I am, or at least, who I was, and go on from there.

On the outside, my life looked successful.

I have always allowed spirit, God, the universe, whatever you want to call it, to lead me, and the direction my life would take. At least I tried. I started reading metaphysical books when I was about 13 and got my first deck of tarot cards at 18. Concepts such as ESP, metaphysics, and personal growth fascinated me. At 30, I found the Berkeley Psychic Institute and studied with them for two years before venturing out on my own, where I created a private practice doing psychic readings and energy healings.

I was again guided to go back to school (I already had my undergraduate degree in Industrial Design) and graduated with an advanced degree as a Naturopathic Physician and finally a Ph.D. in Natural Health Counseling. I have worked for over 20 years as a practicing medical intuitive and energy healer, which has been my full-time source of income. I have helped countless people from around the world find themselves and experience wholeness on physical, mental, emotional, and spiritual levels. Not meaning to be big-headed about it, but I am pretty darn good at what I do.

I have authored five books on a variety of topics, including why we get sick from a subtle energy perspective, energy medicine techniques, ghosts, and the paranormal as well as two books on ancient mysteries. I founded the Institute Of Applied Energetics, which trains individuals to work as an energy medicine practitioner, intuitive counselor, or medical intuitive. I was also the host of a successful internet radio show called Just Energy Radio. I have appeared on radio and television. I was even in a movie and got to see myself up on the big screen.

I have also written countless articles that have appeared in print and online around the globe.

People, who know me, often comment that I always seem grounded. They see me as a kind and loving individual. They suggest that I "fit well into my skin" or that I am authentic because what you see is what you get. Many perceive me as being fearless and suggest that I have the biggest balls of anyone they know. Excuse my French.

It did not start that way for me. I was a child who lived in a constant state of fear. I was just good at covering it up. In the same breath, I would do many other things, even when I was young, that were truly fearless. Climb the three-tiered fence that surrounded the local baseball field at the age of six, no problem. Yet, here we are today, and I think I am going to have to face my biggest fear, my fear of looking deep into my soul and exposing myself to you. So, before I continue, I will take a nice deep breath, ground my body, and go on.

I am not even sure where to start my story. I have experienced so much pain and struggled with boatloads of shame throughout my life. I grew up in a large family. There were eight kids in total – five girls and three boys. I was number three, the rebel, and the "thorn in my mother's side." I grew up believing that there was something inherently wrong with me. At birth, I was born breach and had the umbilical cord wrapped around my neck. My mother would, over the years, remind me that this incident could have left me "retarded."

The dread that I had a severe mental deficiency sat in the background of my young mind. *"What if I was retarded, and no one told me?"* I mean, how would you know if you had a mental challenge while being mentally challenged? My psychological status concerned me significantly, constantly wondering if I were normal, always struggling to be, and act normal.

Dysfunction was rampant in our household. One sister would always make a joke of it, stating how our family *"put the fun in dysfunctional."* We lived in a shame-based home. Its secrets held tighter than all of the gold at Fort Knox. In it, my mom ruled with an iron hand. Infractions of her rules always lead to enormous consequences, ranging from physical, mental to emotional abuse. Her wrath was quick and severe if you did something wrong. My parents did provide us with food, clothing, and shelter, but that was about all we got. They were uninvolved in our lives.

My mom and I had a challenging relationship right from the start. I spend the bulk of my life believing she hated me, that she detested me and that I was the bane of her existence. Some of my earliest memories of my mother are of her beating the daylights out of me. I would hysterically retreat to the only safe place I had. I would climb on my bed and hide. I was little, maybe three years old at the time. I recall many an instance where I would curl up into the tightest ball I could muster, the bedspread over my head. I prayed my mom would not be able to see me. If I could have only disappeared. I knew the small lump sticking out from under the covers would give away my secret.

My Story

I would lay there crying, shaking and hyperventilating, my knees pressed to my chest. I would then try to, what I now know to be self-sooth, endeavoring to calm myself down and shake off the trauma and terror I was experiencing. I was left alone in my pain and misery to get over it. But, the fun did not end there.

There were occasions when I would hear my bedroom door open. In would come my tormentor. Was she going to beat me more? Hadn't she had enough? Curling up into an even tighter ball, my mother would get me out of bed, hold me and profusely apologize. She would tell me over and over that she loved me and that she did not mean to hurt me. I called it the "lovey-dovey story." I did not believe one word she said, and the sad tears that streamed down her cheeks meant nothing to me.

All I could feel in those moments was repulsion for this woman. Her actions showed me just how much she hated me and hated everything about me. I do not understand, even now, why she would tell me the lovey-dovey story. Perhaps she felt guilty for what she had done. Maybe she wanted me to absolve her of her sins. I do not know. I just wanted her to leave me alone. Her words of love were anything but soothing to me.

Do you remember the television show "The Munsters"? It featured the Frankenstein featured Herman Munster and his wife, Lily. One of their commercials featured Eddie, the son of Herman and Lily. He was sitting up in a tree and would not come down. From his perch, he would exclaim, "*Nobody loves me; nobody cares.*" God, I felt like Eddy Munster.

As the years rolled on, we moved from the South Bronx to a house in upstate New York. The physical aggression displayed by my mom diminished. I wrongly assumed the abuse had ended. My mom still hated me, and I was still not sure if my birth trauma had left me retarded or not. I felt pretty smart. I did ok in school. Did my academic achievement indicate that I was normal? The jury was still out.

I am not sure how, when, or why this happened, but as a child, I was excruciatingly shy. If I were around strangers or felt the slightest bit ill at ease, I would not talk. My Uncle Eddy related a story about me when I was young. He recalled situations where I would walk up to a table where people were speaking, stand there for a few moments, and then walk away, never saying a word. I can say this now, but did not understand it at the time; I felt powerless. It took a lot of energy and inner courage to let a fire build in my gut and have words come out of my mouth. At least that is how it felt to me. I also felt worthless. Why would anyone sitting at the table be interested in anything I would have to say? So, I said nothing.

I am bringing this up because this inability to communicate my inner world affected several areas of my life. I was highly sensitive to what was going on around me and would often take on or act out the emotions of everyone in the room. My sensitivity would spike if there were anger, stress, or anxiety present, which did not help my situation.

I was also the family scapegoat. If something unacceptable was going on, all fingers pointed at me, cause it is always Rita's fault. My brothers and sisters would constantly and consistently taunt me. They thought it was funny. They could do it without fear of repercussions. If I did say something, if asked them to stop or screamed at them at the top of my lungs, they would not listen. They would keep going on and on until I was pushed up against a wall, and would lash out with the only thing that stopped them, my fists. That always seemed to work.

My parents only saw, heard about, or perhaps cared about the result. I had gotten physical. Now there was something even wronger with me than my mental retardation. I had a bad temper and was becoming increasingly violent.

I was poked and prodded, psychologically tested, and through my entire sixth-grade year of school, I got to go to counseling – every Tuesday morning. My sessions caused me to miss the early period at school. When my classmates began to inquire where I was and what I was doing, I was instructed to lie. "*I was at the dentist.*" The guilt that I felt, because I deceived my friends, especially while attending a Catholic school, was immense. The added shame I experienced, because now there was undoubtedly something wrong with me, was unbearable.

Counseling was a waste of time. I did not trust the counselor at all. Why would I? Why would I tell some stranger my deepest darkest secrets? I figured that he would turn around and tell all to my parents. I could not imagine the fallout of that. It was not worth going there. I knew anything I did say would be used against me. So, I dutifully sat in the chair every week and watched him clean out his tobacco pipes. I guess it all paid the same.

Then near the end of the school year, my therapist had the bright idea of coming to our house to meeting the whole family. We all sat gathered around the kitchen table. It was not long before my siblings started their incessant torment of me. I wanted to die. It was bad enough when they did it one-on-one, but now I had a whole table full of people belittling and berating me in front of the company. I felt like the sacrificial lamb.

The worst part was that I could not go and smack them for being mean. That would only serve to prove my parent's point, that I was indeed violent. So I just sat there and took it until the visit was over, and the counselor finally left. For whatever reason, I did not have to go back to counseling after that meeting. Maybe he saw what was actually going on and shared his observations with my parents. If I was the counselor, and I observed my brothers' and sisters' behavior towards me, I surely would have. If he did, maybe my parents did not believe what he had to say. Perhaps the whole situation created too much shame for them. So even though my violent tendencies were not miraculously cured, that ended my first round of counseling.

Life continued. It was beyond frustrating. I had no friends and the few people I did manage to befriend, my parents hated. It did not matter who they were. I would inevitably be forbidden to spend time with them. They were all bad influences on me. If there was something I wanted to do, they did not support it, especially if it required any participation on my parent's part.

They kept me under their thumb; their level of control was overwhelming. I was invited to one birthday party the entire time I lived at home. I was so excited because I was asked to attend. Maybe they liked me! It could happen. My delight in the prospect of going was quickly squelched. The battle I fought to go left me emotionally drained. I showed up to the party with bleary red eyes and an embarrassingly inexpensive gift. It was easy to see that I had been crying. I tried to enjoy myself the best that I could, but on the inside, I was an emotional mess.

I obtained a paper route, where I earned about $5.00 per week in ninth grade. While not a lot of money, it offered me the opportunity to invest in myself. My parents terminated my allowance within a week of starting this job. I was "earning my own money now." Instantly I became their slave. I could help cook and clean the house for free.

I was sixteen when theaters released the Exorcist movie. The group of kids (my friends?) I spent time with at school were all talking about going to see it that Friday night. Someone inadvertently asked me if I was going. I was overjoyed. I was invited, right? I asked my parents if I could go. I had zero expectations of them paying for my admission and could have probably found a ride to and from the theater. They said no. Their rationale was that I might go running from the theater scared, into the street, and get hit by a car. WHAT?

Our family always watched sci-fi and horror movies on TV. How could this movie be so scary that I would exhibit this kind of bizarre behavior?

I was devastated, and like the many other times they exerted their control over me, I lost it. Saying I had a hissy fit would be underestimating my reaction. In actuality, it was a full-blown rage attack. It would start with me getting angry. My outburst would result in me being sent to my room. Then the fun would begin. I would scream and yell at the top of my lungs, all the while pounding ferociously on my bedroom door. They did nothing except let me stew in my frustration, which would often trigger me more.

As time progressed, I just started doing what I wanted, which, in all actuality, was not much. I was not a bad kid; I just wanted to have a life, some kind of a life, any kind of life. I concluded it was simpler to ask for forgiveness, deal with the consequences of my actions, and accept the punishment than try to ask for permission. Thankfully, in the few things that I did do, I was never caught.

I felt broken. I knew I was damaged goods. Things were so bad by the time I hit eleventh grade that I went to my guidance counselor and asked her what the best way to commit suicide was. She did nothing. I did, to my chagrin, get to go back to counseling that year — this time, I did share my frustrations about my parents. After a few sessions, the counselor had my parents come in for an appointment. Shockingly, I never went back. My parents started weekly meetings with him instead. I finally felt a small amount of reprieve. Maybe it was not me. Perhaps it was them all along.

I escaped my mother's clutches in January of 1977. A four-year college accepted me for the winter session. It was a full two hundred miles away. I remember counting down the days until I finally could break free of my figurative cage. Tick, tick, tick.

It was getting close to my grand departure date when my mom informed me that if I wanted them to drive me to the campus, I would have to pay for their gas and a night's hotel accommodations. I was shocked. They had close to a full year's advanced notice of my plans. Why were they dumping this on me now? I figured they would be thrilled to finally be getting rid of me. All of their problems would magically go away. I presumed the least they could do would be to drive me up to the school, slow the car down, and push me, and my belongings, out of the door. I would have been okay with that.

The big day came, and my parents graciously drove me down to the bus terminal. I had two giant duffle bags, and my bedding rolled up in tow. It was everything I owned. I purchased a bus ticket and got out of dodge.

The journey to my final destination, my dorm room was arduous. It was a long, long hard day. I was in a strange new city and felt scared and all alone. This experience, however, prepared me on many levels for what would unfold in my life. It was only two years later that I decided to change majors and move across the country to California to attend school. With those same two duffel bags and $125 in my pocket, I boarded a plane and headed out west. Once I got there, I never looked back.

I finally felt free. I sensed an enormous weight lifting off me. The ball and chain that tethered me was gone. I could, at last, be who I wanted to be without fear of repercussions.

Several amazing things happened with my move. I quickly found somewhere to live. By week's end, I had obtained a job. My life started changing rapidly. I had hope for the first time in my life. I was confident that things would be all right.

I also became acutely aware of how dysfunctional I was and realized that I needed healing on multiple levels. I could see that my dreaded fear of communicating with others was also a handicap. I instinctively knew I had to tackle this deficit, so I devised a plan. My first goal was to say hi to the person behind the counter at the convenience mart. I needed to do this before they had the opportunity to greet me. While this might sound like an effortless task to anyone reading these words, it was excruciating for me. I would have to stop before I walked in the store, take a deep breath, suck it up, and proceed inside. It took everything I had to do it. Day by day, this practice got easier.

My first year in California concluded with me receiving my drafting certification and obtaining a good-paying job. I graduated from college a few years later, which was a painful process all by itself, but I did it. I was confident and self-assured, and felt like a normal person. It was amazing.

My Story

I also spent a lot of time reading metaphysical and self-help books as part of my healing plan. One day, during this period, I had a revelation that was even more remarkable. I ascertained that I was not a violent, angry person. I had not had one of yelling, screaming, and pounding on doors bouts since I had moved out of my parents' house. I had not hit anyone. I had not experienced the level of rage I had come to know earlier in my life even once. I was, in reality, a laid-back person for the most part. Imagine that!

My life seemed to be moving forward positively, well, at least externally. Looked good, felt good, was financially stable, and was, for anyone looking in from the outside, successful. I had books, clients, fans, and followers. What more could you ask for?

Oh yea, how about happiness?

Fast forward, many years, several marriages, and many long-term relationships later. It is December of 2018, the week before Christmas. I had just caught my then live-in boyfriend sneaking alcohol into the house and drinking again. Despite multiple threats, me begging and pleading with him to get help, nothing had changed. I was at my wit's end, and he just placed the straw that broke this camel's back. It was not only his secretive drinking that concerned me. There seemed to be something fundamentally wrong with him.

His behavior was erratic. A simple question or innocent comment would set him off into some weird delusional place, a place that he would often live in for days. Then the fun would begin. I spent my days and nights walking around on eggshells. Whenever I would put my foot down and threaten to kick him out, he would seem to open up, acknowledge his shortcomings, and promise to do something about it. Promise, yes, do something about it, no.

It became evident that he did not care about my wants and needs. Then on that fateful day, I busted him with yet another bottle of booze. I was done. It did not matter to me that he had wrecked his car months before and according to him, was not drivable. It was not my problem that he did not do anything to repair it. It was also not my problem that he had no major credit cards, so he could not get a rental. He had to go. Somehow, through some kind of divine intervention, his car worked well enough for him to make it out of my driveway and out of my life.

I do not mean to drag out this part of the story, but it is critical in understanding what happened next.

I contacted him once he was gone, regarding the rest of his belonging that were still in my house. I wanted to know when he was going to pick them up. His response was, "*I'll try to come by and get them as soon as possible.*" I knew his reply was secret code, meaning do not hold your breath. Since the mountain was not coming to Mohammad, I enlisted a good friend with a truck to help me take his remaining things to him.

I decided to be dropped off at a nearby restaurant while the truck and his things continued to their final destination. I sat and awaited my friend's return. This is where things got beyond odd from a synchronicity perspective. My cell phone

My Story

chimed. It was a message from one of my ex-husband's current wife, a woman whom I had only spoken to once in the past. Why would she be reaching out to me?

Her message stated something to the effect that she had been noticing some patterns in my ex's behavior and wanted to see if I had experienced the same kinds of issues with him. Ok, I was intrigued. He was a piece of work. Interestingly, his behavior on many levels was reflective of the relationship I was ending. Suffice it to say they shared an excessive number of characteristics that were challenging.

We connected on the phone later that day. The first thing that came out of her mouth, after a few general pleasantries, was "*he's a narcissist.*" My whole world changed in that instant. I had just been reading material about that very topic, noticing how very narcissistic my current, now ex-beau had been. Her disclosure turned what I thought had been about me and my imagination into something up close and personal. My mind started reeling. It caused me to stop and look long and hard at my life.

I was shocked.

What I came to realize was the scary fact that the majority of my intimate relationships were abusive. I kept going back in time, evaluating each of my romantic interactions until I reached my family of origin. Wow! I came to discover that the abuse had not ended with the physical beatings from my mother. I also found that my parents were great teachers, and over the years, they had provided me with an excellent education, an education only an abuser can offer. It was more than I could envision.

They taught me that I did not matter. They taught me that people did not like me, let alone myself. They taught me that I was inherently flawed and internally broken. They taught me I did not have a choice. They taught me how to take on all of the responsibilities while having no power to change it. They taught me that love meant giving up on myself, an act inextricably tied to how much I was willing to tolerate. Yes, I had a Ph.D. in standing there and silently taking it. I made an excellent punching bag, figuratively speaking, and a willing victim for people who were interested in sucking me dry.

Don Ruiz, in his book *The Four Agreements*, tells us:

In your whole life nobody has ever abused you more than you have abused yourself. And the limit of your self-abuse is exactly the limit that you will tolerate from someone else. If someone abuses you a little more than you abuse yourself, you will probably walk away from that person. But if someone abuses you a little less than you abuse yourself, you will probably stay in the relationship and tolerate it endlessly.

If you abuse yourself very badly, you can even tolerate someone who beats you up, humiliates you, and treats you like dirt. Why? Because in your belief system you say, "I deserve it. This person is doing me a favor by being with me. I'm not worthy of love and respect. I'm not good enough.

It was like a giant band-aid was ripped off my preverbal third eye. I can only guess I needed neon lights, warning

My Story

sirens, and a massive whack up the side of my head to finally see the dysfunctional pattern that had plagued every one of my relationships. I had finally gotten the message. It was time for me to tackle the deepest, most entrenched, and ugliest parts of myself, my core beliefs.

It is from this place that I started digging into the dynamics of empaths and narcissists. I began to see the patterns of abuse I had learned to tolerate over the years. I was finally able to put words to my experiences. It validated so much. It took what had happened to me from some vague "thing" looming in the background and made it real, painful, but real. I had been oblivious to what was going on right in front of my face. As intuitive and as self-reflecting as I am, I did not see it.

For me, I guess I did not understand two basic concepts. One; that it is my job to make me happy. When you are anxious, stressed, and walking around on eggshells, you are getting a clear indicator that you are not content. The second concept was the notion of choice. I could choose! You do not know how happy I was to hear those words. I had a choice, and through this choice, I could control my emotional destiny. Thus began the journey to healing, one that I am going to share with you.

I am going to leave my story off here, at least for now. Did I tell all, no. I think with the little that I have shared, you have an idea of my history. I hope that as you continue reading, you will garner a better understanding of who you are, what you have, or may be currently experiencing in your life. Perhaps by putting these words forward and revealing my life, my truth, with you, you might be spared the pain and trauma of ongoing, repeated dysfunctional relationships. They say knowledge is power. By understanding what was, has, or is happening to you, this increased awareness might support you as you break free from patterns of abuse.

The Many Shades Of Abuse

Our childhood experiences are fundamental to our emotional development. These experiences set the tone of our lives and form the foundation of how we act and react in every situation we encounter. Our emotions start to develop in the womb and continue until we reach the age of 12. During our formative years, our parents play a pivotal role in how we experience the world. Through them, we learn to determine what is safe from what is not.

Parenting, in general, is a complex juggling act. It is a parent's job to teach and guide their children into the ways of the world and the rules prescribed by society. Humans, said plainly, are a domesticated species. Our parents teach us the skills required to survive in polite society. It is our parent's job to teach us good from bad, and right from wrong. They show us these things through a variety of rewards and punishments. When we learn to say "*Ma Ma*" or "*Da Da*", we are praised and encouraged. Discipline, on the other hand, is employed if we do something that breaks one of our parent's rules. We are a bad boy or a bad girl. This training leads to socialization and successful functioning in today's society. This kind of enculturation happens in every civilization on the planet and IS what makes us intrinsically human.

Children, by nature, can be loud and unruly. These behaviors can cause parents to feel irritated, annoyed, or frustrated. If a parent engages in the challenges of parenthood from an unhealthy place, from a place of power and control over their children, anger or fear, abuse can follow. They might take their displaced feelings out on the innocent youth, utilizing whatever means necessary to maintain control.

Would it surprise you to discover that the emotional scars that formed due to adverse life experiences are still affecting you today? Many of us are entirely unaware of how these early life events are influencing us. If the abuse was overt and tangible, such as in physical or sexual abuse, we might assume that once the mistreatment ran its course, or our situation changed, we can merrily go on with our lives. We may believe everything is all right. Silly us.

Mental and emotional abuse, as well as neglect, is hard to spot. This entrenched trauma leaves no scars, but its effects on the developing child are immense. Victims of childhood abuse often experience serious consequences later on in life. Its aftereffects can rear its ugly head and wreak havoc in all of their relations, especially their most intimate ones. Children who experience abuse are more likely to have lifelong problems building and maintaining relationships, especially healthy ones.

Hard as this may be to hear, the people we associate with and have close connections to, reflect our inner world. If we are confident and have a positive self-image, we tend to attract individuals who reflect these characteristics. If instead, our inner world is somehow lacking, we will generally attract negative and potentially parasitic people into our lives. These individuals can include close friends and intimate partners. Many survivors find themselves becoming involved with people who are narcissistic, abusive, or emotionally unavailable. They are a magnet for unhealthy partners and cannot understand why.

It all goes back to our upbringing. How abuse survivors interpret what is healthy and normal in a relationship is often distorted. They may accept poor behavior and assume this is how life is supposed to be between two loving people. It is not because they are inviting abuse into their lives, but more often than not, they do not know any better.

Physiological Impact Of Abuse

Trauma can have more than emotional and psychological effects on us. It can have physiological consequences, as well. When we sense danger, the sympathetic nervous system activates, which automatically triggers a stress response. It is sometimes called our "fear response" or our "fight or flight mechanism." Our stress response prepares our bodies to deal with perceived or real emergencies by releasing hormones (adrenaline, cortisol, norepinephrine, and others) into the bloodstream. It brings about specific physiological, psychological, and emotional changes all in an attempt to survive. This flood of stress hormones heightens our awareness; elevates our heart rate, constricts our blood vessels, stimulates our nervous system, alters our brain and digestive function, and changes our breathing rate.

If an infant, small child, or even a teen, perceives the world as a scary place, is consistently and repeatedly frightened, or cannot count on a level of consistency in their environment, they can develop a brain and body system, which is constantly on guard and on hyper-alert. Children have no choice but to deal with the dynamics of what goes on inside in a highly stressful home. They cannot run, flee, or fight back. They are victims of their circumstances and have no control over the outcome. Many times they do not have a safe place to land, be soothed, and recover from what they encountered.

According to Harvard University's Center on the Developing Child article entitled *Toxic Stress*:

> Toxic stress response can occur when a child experiences strong, frequent, and/or prolonged adversity -- such as physical or emotional abuse, chronic neglect, caregiver substance abuse or mental illness, exposure to violence, and/or the accumulated burdens of family economic

> hardship -- *without adequate adult support. This kind of prolonged activation of the stress response systems can disrupt the development of brain architecture and other organ systems, and increase the risk for stress-related disease and cognitive impairment, well into the adult years.*

The troubled child's ability to address or adapt to stress often becomes maladjusted. The constant tension in their toxic homes can cause the child to sense threats everywhere. These ongoing fears can chronically trigger a child's stress response causing it to work on overdrive, sometimes without a chance to relax. It can affect the way the brain develops by creating neural pathways that shape the way the adult child reacts to seeming threats as well as their ability to recover from a stressful event.

This stress response pattern may have been functional when young, but later in life, it may interfere in their ability to take action healthily. It lays dormant within the psyche until triggered by life events. These responses are, on many levels, hardwired into the brain. It is where the mind and body automatically, and reflexively will go when it senses a threat. For years, it was all that kept them alive.

The aftereffect of long-termed abuse can be painful and emotionally traumatic. Adult children may grow up to be routinely anxious and fearful, awaiting doom and gloom around every corner. They may have problems with emotional regulation. They may lash out in anger if triggered or retreat and withdraw into themselves. They may have difficulties in their friendships or long-term relationships. They may have trust issues. They may see themselves as unworthy, have low self-esteem, or even blame themselves for the abuse they suffered. They may have learned to deny their feelings or have an instilled belief that they do not matter. They may develop substance abuse disorders, PTSD, or an acute stress disorder. A personality disorder such as borderline, narcissistic, or histrionic personality disorders or a dissociative identity disorder (formally known as multiple personality disorder) might emerge if the abuse started at an early age.

If you are reading this book, you may have uncovered the fact that you are a survivor of abuse or neglect. Maybe you have conscious recollections of it. Perhaps traumatic memories surfaced spontaneously or while in therapy. You may find yourself at a place in your life where you are ready to heal the layers of ingrained pain, suffering, and trauma you encountered as a child. It is only by unfolding who you are and where you came from that you can start to understand why you react the way you do. This understanding can help people, like you, who came from a toxic home environment, gain insights into their origins. It may also provide you with the opportunity to begin the healing process and break free of the chronic and ongoing cycle of dysfunction that is controlling your life.

As we move forward through this section, take the time to reflect on your own childhood experiences. Something discussed may hit a resonating cord within your being. You can use the space provided at the end of each topic to keep track of what you may have discovered about yourself. *"How did I get to this place?" "What factors were involved?" "How have the things I have gone through in my early life affected me as an adult?"* These steps toward self-discovery will help you to understand yourself and your hidden motivations. This insight will also provide you with a foundation for change.

So take a deep breath and turn the page. Open yourself up to discovering the real you!

Was I Abused?

The definition of abuse is a pattern of behavior used by one person that causes harm to another. The harsh tactics utilized are often employed to gain and maintain power over another, and in this instance, a child. A onetime situation, such as paddling a child's bottom for a flagrant transgression, does not qualify as abuse. Abuse is an act that is repeated and has appeared multiple times in an individual's life, if not daily.

The line is clear for some people as to what is and what is not considered abuse. It is never appropriate, for example, to have sexual contact with a child. There are many instances where the line is less obvious. Separating what proper discipline or child-rearing strategies are from what is abusive can be tricky, especially when viewed through a child's eyes.

Physical trauma is what most people think of when they hear the word abuse. This is not the case. Abuse comes in a variety of forms, including sexual, verbal, or emotional abuse. Witnessing cruelty in cases of domestic violence is also identified as a form of child abuse. Neglect, the lack of love, care, and attention for a child, can damage a child just as much as any other form of maltreatment. Sadly, children who grow up in toxic households become accustomed to varying levels of abuse. The treatment they experience is seen as commonplace and do not recognize the injury they have just encountered.

If you are unsure if you are the victim of abuse, here is a simple checklist you can use to assess your life. As you evaluate the items on the list, do not consider a once-off situation but instead look for repeated patterns of negative parental behavior. If you find yourself answering yes to several items on this list, then perhaps you are a survivor of abuse.

Tell-tale Signs Of Abuse

Has one or both parents regularly or routinely:

- Hit or harmed you in any way?
- Threatened to hurt or kill you?
- Forced you to have sex with him or her or another individual? (Sexual contact with a minor is abuse even if this only happens once.)
- Threatened to destroy your personal property and possessions?
- Disregard your opinions, ideas, suggestions, or needs?
- Made you feel bad about yourself or put you down?
- Belittled and trivialized you, your accomplishments, or your hopes and dreams?
- Made fun of you, and caused you to feel shame or embarrassment?
- Pointed out your flaws, mistakes, or shortcomings?
- Made you endure physical closeness that you did not want?
- Crossed your boundaries?

- Called you names, criticized you harshly, or made cutting remarks under their breath?
- Acted emotionally distant or emotionally unavailable most of the time?
- Disregard your feelings?
- Yelled or screamed at you or flew into a rage?
- Made you feel guilty for being your authentic self or not appreciate you for who you were?
- Stifled your decisions, even when you were old enough to decide on your own?
- Made you feel guilty for doing what you wanted and not what they wanted?

Any of these things alone, or in combination, can leave a negative impression on a child's psyche. We can wear our trauma on our shirtsleeves, where everyone can see our dysfunction, or we can bury it into the deep dark recesses of our minds. That is, until something happens and triggers us, and our bodies automatically respond. But first things first. Let us dig into how we might have gotten into this situation in the first place by taking a long hard look at our parents or caregivers.

The Many Shades Of Abuse

How did you do?
What behaviors did your parents/caregiver display?

Parenting Styles

The strategy our parents used to raise us and help us assimilate into society vary greatly. A parenting style is a series of categories used by psychologists to identify the way adults traditionally rear their children. Each type describes a set of practices a parent may employ. The four primary parenting styles include: authoritarian, permissive, uninvolved, and authoritative.

Authoritarian Parents

Characteristics of the authoritarian parenting style encompass a life filled with rules with little parental responsiveness. Parental responsiveness referrers to the degree in which a parent reacts to the child's needs in an accepting and supportive manner. Authoritarian parents seldom show warmth toward their children and are often cold and harsh. They lack patience and value discipline over fun.

Authoritarian parents expect absolute and unquestioning obedience. In this family dynamic, you do not question authority. Obeying orders, without explanation, is required. Punishment is always swift and decisive. These parents believe it is their responsibility to bend the child's will, so it coincides with the established rules and regulations. Willfulness is not allowed. Negotiation is non-existent. Feedback, from the child, is scorned. Authoritarian parents place little or no value on their child's point of view.

These parents attempt to exert control over every aspect of their child's life. Their monikers are "because I said so," "it's my way or the highway," or "suck it up." They like to use fear and harsh punishment, with little or no explanation, as a way to control behaviors when they do not meet expectations or their host of unwritten rules. In many instances, the child is expected to be a mind reader knowing these rules exist or should simply know better. The authoritarian parenting style is the most controlling form and can often devolve into abuse, especially if the parent tends to overreact negatively when a child breaks a directive.

Permissive Parents

Permissive parents, sometimes called indulgent parents, are the least demanding but are very responsive to the child's needs. They are warm and loving to their children and want them to be happy. Permissive parents have a hard time saying "*No.*" They avoid exerting their power and authority. They tend to utilize gift-giving and enticement, versus boundaries and expectations, as their primary parenting tools.

They make little or no attempt to control or discipline their offspring. These parents are lenient, avoid confrontation, and rarely make or enforce rules and guidelines. This parenting style provides little structure for their children. The child is required to regulate his or her behavior and is left to figure things out for themselves. Responsibilities, demands, and expectations are low. Their moniker is "kids will be kids." They tend to be more like a friend to a child than an authority figure. Children of permissive parents often have issues taking responsibility or lack a strong internal compass. They may also find themselves lacking self-confidence or are more vulnerable to peer influences.

Uninvolved Parents

Uninvolved parents are not demanding and lack responsiveness to their child's needs. Uninvolved parents might meet that child's basic needs for food and shelter, but often believe this is where their duties end. They practice a hands-off parenting style where they, on some levels, expect their children to raise themselves. They are often self-centered, indifferent, dismissive, or downright neglectful. They do not devote much of time or energy into their child's emotional needs, especially in the way of guidance or affection.

Many times the neglect experienced by these children is not intentional. Uninvolved parents are often busy with work commitments, activities, or other life issues. They can be so wrapped up in their personal affairs that they fail to recognize or notice the needs and concerns of their offspring. Sometimes they are overwhelmed by the tasks required to survive day to day. Mental health or substance abuse issues may also factor in these parent's inability to care for their children. Children raised by indifferent parents have some of the worst psychological adjustment second only to hostile or abusive parenting.

Authoritative Parents

Authoritative parents have high standards and expectations of their children, which is tempered by their being responsive to their child's needs. These parents, while setting limits, provide their children a warm, loving, and nurturing environment. They listen to their children and offer them the support they need.

Authoritative parents, like authoritarian parents, expect their children to obey their rules and behave appropriately. How the authoritative parent addresses discipline, however, is vastly different. Authoritative parents typically set clear and achievable limits. They use reason, negotiation, and discussion to teach their children what they require of them and back up their rules by enforcing consistent boundaries. They are firm when disciplining but are not mean or emotionally reactive when a child disobeys.

Authoritative parents do not try to control their children and expect them to obey blindly like an authoritarian parent. This parenting style allows their children to act independently, supporting self-esteem and confidence while providing them with a safety net for the times they may fall and falter. This parenting style is the most effective method of child-rearing and tends to produce well-adjusted, confident, and successful kids.

Inside A Parent's Mind: What Were They Thinking?

There are several theories about why a parent would travel down a path of abuse. Some parents never wanted children but brought them into the world out of a sense of duty, obligation, or to fulfill their role in society. These individuals are typically not interested in putting in the time or energy required for successful parenting. Many parents are unprepared for their role as a caregiver. They might not have the skills needed to do the job correctly. They may suffer some form of substance abuse or have a mental health issue that interferes with their ability to interact with their children appropriately. They might lack family or community support or feel overwhelmed with the tasks required of them.

Some parents are survivors of an abusive upbringing themselves. They, because of their life experience, developed an abnormal perspective of violence and healthful child-rearing. They may take on the belief that sparing the rod spoils the child. They may perceive the unhealthy behaviors they experienced as a child as the correct and perhaps only way of raising children. Children raised by dysfunctional parents learn that abuse is a normal part of intimate relationships and family dynamics. They often never learn healthy ways of dealing with conflict and conflict resolution. This type of conditioning is habitually passed down from one generation to the next.

Sometimes early childhood trauma can leave a child with a sense of vulnerability and powerlessness. When these victimized children grow into adulthood and have a family of their own, they may, in a hope to regain the power they lost, mimic, or copy the same behaviors they experienced. They go from victim to perpetrator, and the cycle of abuse continues.

Studies indicate that mothers are more likely to neglect their children. They are often the primary caregiver and are typically responsible for the day-to-day tasks associated with child rearing. These everyday duties can overwhelm the caregiver, where they spend all of their time and energy getting the job done. The parent may also be extremely task-focused. In either case, there is no room for the child and the child's need, who, in the end, tends to be neglected and ignored.

Was it one overriding issue or a combination of factors that aligned into the perfect storm that you called your formative years?

Take a few moments to identify your parent's parenting style.

What parenting style did your parents employ?

Inside The Abused Mind

Our parents are our primary point of contact and context when we first entered this world. Since we were not mentally and emotionally mature, we believed what they told us. We receive their messages both verbally and through their actions. These messages form the foundation of how we view the world.

As children, we do not have the information or skills required to determine the reality or fallacy of a belief or belief system. We are children! We do not know any better. We accept what we see, feel, and experience as factual. We never question the integrity of what our parents are teaching us.

Programmed beliefs underscore the issues associated with individuals who discriminate based upon race, creed, or color or sexual preference. True, as well as false beliefs, are instilled into us, right, wrong, or indifferent. Many times people carry limiting beliefs without an understanding of why they feel the way they feel, or act the way they do.

Individuals who suffer at the hands of abuse or neglect, often suffer from destructive unconscious programs that can infiltrate every fiber of their being. The seeds of false beliefs, planted during childhood, can be likened to the branches of a tree. The seed, once germinated, starts to develop. They, like the tree, grow larger each time one of our negative viewpoints is triggered and reinforced. New branches form with each traumatic event we encounter. The tree keeps growing, and eventually, we can only see the world through its dense foliage. We hold these beliefs so close we often assume this is who we are.

For our purposes, we will be focusing on two distinct areas: attachment styles and core beliefs. Combined, they set the stage of how we see our encounters with others and ourselves. They create the foundational pattern we use to navigate life and play an active role in all of our relationships.

Early Attachment Patterns

An emotional attachment is a bond we form with other people. They identify how we relate to others. When this bond is between a parent and a child, the dynamics experienced can influence the quality of our adult relationships, especially when dealing with intimacy, conflict, or stress. Our attachment style forms during the first two years of our lives. If an infant's needs are responded to appropriately, a secure attachment style develops. Our psyche can suffer emotional limitation and psychological impairment if our caregiver is not attuned to us.

There are four primary attachment styles: secure, dismissive-avoidant, anxious-preoccupied, and fearful-avoidant. Each has different developmental causes and express themselves in a unique set of internal beliefs and triggering behaviors. Dr. Phillip Shaver and Dr. Cindy Hazan, in their research suggest that we exhibit the same attachment patterns with our romantic partner as we developed as an infant. By understanding your style of attachment, you may gain insights into how you developed emotionally and how you may still be acting and reacting in adulthood.

Secure Attachment Style

Individuals develop a secure attachment style when their caregiver was sensitive and responsive to their needs and fulfills them. When a child cries or otherwise expresses a need, the parent responds healthily. The child may be spoken to, picked up, or in some way reassured. These well-nurtured children received a consistent level of care and attention, which leaves them feeling seen, safe, and soothed.

As an adult, individuals with a secure attachment have a favorable view of themselves and their relationships. They feel confident that people are there for them when they are needed. They are independent and self-assured. They tend to be relaxed and not anxious in their relationships. They can express their needs and feelings to their partners. In turn, they can listen to and be responsive to their partner's needs as well.

Dismissive-Avoidant Attachment Style

Children develop the dismissive-avoidant attachment style when a caretaker is unresponsive to their needs. These children grow up with a subconscious fear of intimacy. They value independence and may see dependent people as weak. They do not like to have strings attached or to be tied down without an escape route in sight. They will avoid anything that could interfere with their autonomy at all costs.

These individuals learned from the time they were infants to disconnect from their bodies and minimize their emotions. They tend to repress rather than express their feeling, mainly when their attachment needs are triggered. In a crisis, they will not ask for help. If looked at from the outside, they seem self-reliant and do not present signs of vulnerability. They can carry the air of being able to take care of life's challenges all by themselves. When they do need help, they will use indirect strategies such as hinting, sulking, or complaining to get their needs met.

The dismissive-avoidant tends to be a loner. They may desire to have a close relationship, but the closer a partner gets, the more dismissive they can become. They may reject or withdraw when his or her partner asks for more intimacy or attention. They might resort to deactivating strategies to create space between themselves and the object of their stress. A deactivating strategy is a thought or behavior that pulls in the reins on the relationship. They may view their partner as wanting too much or as being clingy. They might find small faults in them. They may retreat into work or other intellectual pursuits. They tend to go into this reactive posturing when a relationship becomes too close, or you threaten their independence.

Individuals with a dismissive-avoidant attachment style typically attract partners who do not want to help meet their needs, preferring the independence the dismissive naturally desires. They might form relationships with unavailable people, such as a married person.

Anxious Preoccupied Attachment Style

Children who develop an anxious preoccupied attachment style spend their early life confused regarding what kind of nurturing they will receive. The parenting these children receive is inconsistent. At times, the parent or caregiver is responsive to the child's needs, and at other times, they are insensitive or neglectful of them. The unpredictability of the caregiver will leave the child distrustful and insecure. Unlike dismissive-avoidant children who cope by becoming self-reliant and independent, these children can act desperate and clingy.

As an adult, these individuals often experience anxiety in their relationships. They worry about being rejected and abandoned, which can lead to clinginess, possessiveness, and jealousy. They worry that if they do not satisfactorily meet the other person's needs, the relationship will be over, and their partner will move on. This fear causes them to be vigilant in trying to figure out what they can do to make their partner love them.

Their self-critical nature and deep-seated self-doubt cause them to seek reassurance and approval regularly. They do not believe they are good enough, which makes it hard for them to trust that they are loved. This limiting belief infiltrates all of their relationships. They may attract someone inconsistent in showing affection or meeting their needs. They may also form a relationship with someone more dominant or critical of who they are. When they do not get the reassurance they need, they can become angry or resentful. They may also resort to manipulation to have their needs met.

Fearful Avoidant Attachment Style

Infants have an intrinsic need to feel safe and supported by their parents or caregiver. But what happens if the person the child wants to go to for comfort and reassurance is also the person they fear? This enigma leaves the child in a terrible dilemma. The person whom they feel they should be able to rely on is also the source of their most significant distress. The child is forced to endure a no-win situation. They realize early on that they will not get their needs met without experiencing terror at the same time. They will never be safe.

This scenario causes the child to disassociate from his or her body. This coping mechanism allows the youth to detach from what is going on around them, often blocking the experience from their consciousness. They do not just hide from the pain or bury their emotions; they disconnected from them completely.

The fearful-avoidant attachment style, sometimes referred to as anxious-avoidant or disorganized, is a combination of both the dismissive-avoidant and anxious preoccupied attachment styles. They distrust their caregivers, like a dismissive-avoidant, but have low self-esteem and a negative view of themselves, like the anxious-preoccupied who wants and needs intimacy.

Fearful avoidants can feel a desperate, overwhelming need to be in a relationship. This initial connection makes them feel safe. As a relationship deepens, their fears and mistrust of being let down begin to surface, causing them to withdraw and distance themselves. They anticipate rejection, betrayal, and hurt. They never feel safe, which leaves them on constant alert waiting for the next shoe to drop or some terrible thing to happen.

Many times, fearful-avoidant individuals have problems with emotional regulation and controlling their stress levels. They believe people are out to get them and have no coping mechanism for dealing with these internal fears. Their remedy to this discomfort is to lash out. They may act hostile or aggressive, particularly when their anxiety is triggered.

They can also have a hard time communicating and expressing their emotions. Receiving affection is challenging, as well. They may not trust where the warmth is coming from or may not believe that they deserve any in the first place. Sadly, individuals with this attachment style typically attracted people who are neglectful or abusive.

Can you identify your attachment style?

Core Or Limiting Beliefs

Core beliefs establish the foundation of how we see ourselves, others, the world around us, and our perceived future. They are like a computer program on our internal hard drive that shapes and formulates all of the information we process. Core beliefs form as a result of our early childhood interactions, significant life events, inherited mindsets, and cultural influences. Some core beliefs serve us well. Others do not. They can be entrenched so deeply into our psyches that many times, we do not know they are even there.

Limiting core beliefs, like any core belief, sit in the background of our consciousness and underlie many of our automatic thoughts and emotional reactions. We often assume this is who we are. We may believe that we are ugly, stupid, unlovable, flawed, broken, or just not good enough. Deep down, we may conclude that we do not matter or are worthless. These beliefs affect our self-esteem and can cause a litany of other issues.

The effect of the negative beliefs we carry can take on many forms. They may cause us to neglect ourselves. We may withdraw into ourselves. We may not speak up and express our wants and needs. Instead of becoming quiet, we might take on the opposite extreme, where we react inappropriately. We may get loud, dramatic, or explosive as a way of expressing our feelings.

Negative core beliefs often surface in individuals who grew up in toxic households. They include but are not limited to, abandonment, defectiveness, subjugation, dependency, and entitlement. We used these self-limiting scripts to help us survive our childhood experiences, cope with life, and attempt to get our needs met.

If we could only hit the delete button and magically wipe our inner slate clean. Many of our negative beliefs are so integrated into our personalities; we could not imagine what life would be like without them. Their chronic and insidious nature is a gift that keeps on giving, that is until we decide to change them.

Abandonment

Loss underlies our fear of being abandoned. Our first abandonment experience may occur at birth when we emerge from the warm comfort of our mother's womb into a strange, unfamiliar world. This transition is scary enough. If you were born in a hospital during the mid-1900s, this is where the fun began. Welcome to the world and midcentury delivery practices.

The umbilical cord, the connection between the mother and the newborn child, is cut just after delivery. The newborn has to become accustomed to breathing air for the first time quickly. Some infants may feel like they are suffocating from lack of oxygen and internalize a belief they have to fight for their lives.

The child, once delivered, was automatically taken from the mother. Its nose and mouth suctioned to clear out mucus. They may put stinging antiseptic drops into his or her eyes. If the baby does not start crying on its own, it may be suspended in the air, held upside-down, and spanked. The child would then be cleaned up, wrapped up, sent to the nursery, and put on display with all of the other newborns.

If that was not bad enough, it was also a common practice to drug the mother. This procedure left her unconscious and unable to participate in the birth of her child. The narcotics she received would pass through the umbilical cord, drugging the unborn child as well. The distressed child, once born, would have to wait for his or her mother to regain consciousness. It was only then that they would be able to reconnect with the only person they have known for the past nine months. It is no wonder why we are so messed up.

Add to this, if there were any additional birth complications such as being born breach, having the cord wrapped around your neck, having forceps used during delivery or being delivered by cesarean section, the level of trauma the child experiences increases. The birthing process is, for many, the original wounding.

The doctors at the time did not take notice of the person inside the little body. They assumed that their actions, and the subsequent trauma they caused, would not register in the child's brain and would be quickly forgotten. Thankfully, birth and delivery practices have evolved over the last few years, which should significantly reduce the effects of birth trauma and the abandonment associated with it.

The reality is, we all experience loss and rejection growing up. These losses can be severe, like the loss of a parent through death or divorce. A dysfunctional relationship between a parent and a child, where physical and emotional abuse, neglect, or an unavailable caregiver leaves the child feeling unsafe, can also produce feelings of profound loss. The child can grow up feeling insecure and distrustful.

Abandonment fear can be overpowering. When triggered, it can activate our stress response and bring back the same feelings we experienced when we were children. The reaction these deep-seated fears create can get right in the middle of having a healthy adult relationship. Individuals who suffer from a subconscious fear of abandonment tend to have low self-esteem and are self-deprecating. They may respond inappropriately to criticism or at the slightest thought of rejection. They may have a hard time trusting, suffer from chronic feelings of insecurity, and even depression. They may have intrusive negative thoughts and excessive worry. They might experience debilitating anxiety, have panic attacks, or feel the need to self-medicate. They may be needy and clingy or, when triggered, become emotionally distant and numb. As an adult, they may form relationships with people who are unavailable to them.

Defectiveness

When someone believes they are defective, they internalize the notion that they are fundamentally flawed, broken, incompetent, inadequate, or inferior. These individuals may feel unworthy or hold the underlying belief they are unlovable. They may, at their core, believe that they are so imperfect that no matter what they say or do, it will always be wrong. They may also worry that people will discover their inherent brokenness, which can bring up intense feelings of shame. They may conclude, "*If my parents could not love me, there really must be something wrong with me.*"

These individuals may see themselves as too needy, ugly, dumb, strange, or controlling. Almost any aspect of their personality can be flagged as being defective. They tend to compare themselves with others who they see as "normal" and then beat themselves up for areas in which they fall short. They assume that people will always see them in a negative light and experience extreme fear, shame, and embarrassment. They live in fear and anticipation of exposing their actual selves. Their internal dialog may sound something like:

- I'm not good enough.
- I can't do anything right.
- There's something wrong with me.
- I'm weird.
- I'm stupid.
- I'm worthless.
- I'm bad.

- I'm fat.
- I'm ugly.
- I'm a failure.

Subjugation

The term subjugation refers to the act or process of bringing someone or something under one's control. It is a form of mental enslavement. Individuals who have the core belief of subjugation are people who have issues asserting themselves, establishing boundaries, expressing their feelings, or dealing with conflict. They are the ultimate people pleasers.

People who have subjugation (people-pleasing) as their core belief are often loyal and responsible. They are diligent and dependable, helpful and hardworking, courteous and considerate, generous and accommodating. Deep down, however, they believe that they are responsible for the happiness of others. This belief tricks them into using their time and energy to help those in need, many times, to their detriment.

These individuals often experience fear and anxiety when expressing their feelings or when establishing boundaries. They worry that there will be some form of retaliation, rejection, or they will not be able to cope with the outcome if they exert themselves. The fear, anxiety, and worry of standing up for themselves often cause them to fold, forcing them to accept or do things they do not want to do. People with this core belief have a hard time saying, "*No*."

The Many Shades Of Abuse

If you were mistreated as a child or grew up in a house where it was dangerous to express your feelings or speak up, you are very likely to have this core belief embedded within you. Some children who have subjugation as a core belief found that rewards or approval only occurred when they met the needs of their parents. Others may have complied with their parents desires because they felt like they had no choice. They learned early on that "resistance was futile" and non-conformity only meant they would have to suffer the consequences. If a child did manage to assert his or her will, it was typically responded to negatively with disapproval, rejection, abandonment, or punishment. In the end, the child learned that it was in his or her best interests to swallow their emotions and stay quiet rather than risk parental repercussions.

People who suffer from this core belief are great at nurturing those around them but do not know how to take care of and nurture themselves. They focus on gratifying everyone else's needs before their own. They do this for two very distinct reasons. The subjugated person may allow others to dominate them and surrender out of fear of punishment or retaliation. These individuals often felt bullied or powerless as children. They give up on themselves and internalize their needs, not because they should, but because they had no other choice. Their motivation to serve does not come from a sincere desire to help but rather from a fear of retribution.

The self-sacrificing individual, on the other hand, is hyper-focused on pleasing others and gratifying their needs before their own. Internally, they believe it is bad or wrong to express their feelings and often feel ashamed or guilty when they do. These individuals may exhibit this behavior because they do not want those close to them to experience any discomfort. They may believe it is the right thing to do or because they want to maintain a connection with someone. These individuals tend to be highly empathic and are often acutely aware of the pain of others, so aware that they are often motivated to prevent or alleviate it. This internal dynamic often plays a significant role in co-dependent behaviors.

In a relationship, these individuals have a hard time speaking their minds. They prefer to get along with everyone and avoid conflict. This characteristic leaves them appearing indecisive or lacking initiative. They fear that their opinions will be at odds with others, and believe expressing them will cause trouble. They may internalize concepts such as *"if I am nice to him, he won't leave me"* or *"if I am nice to her and do all of these things for her, she will love me."* Many times they see it as the only way to gain their partners' attention and affection. Many times their needs and desires are so repressed that they do not know what they want.

Individuals who have this unresolved core belief tend to attract dominating, parasitic, or manipulative people who mirror their original patterns of parental abuse. Their need to prove their worth can lead to physical and emotional burnout since they do not know how to or cannot let themselves relax. Their one-way drive can also lead to increased resentment in the relationship and manifest as explosive outbursts or as passive-aggressive behaviors.

Dependency

We all need to be able to rely on others or at times, be taken care of. This kind of assistance feels good and is nurturing to our souls. In a healthy relationship, there should be a give and take of support, an ebb, and flow, an equal exchange of energy. This dynamic is called interdependence, and it is a beautiful thing.

For someone whose core beliefs revolve around dependency, they may think they are helpless, powerless, lack control, cannot adequately handle things, or take care of themselves. They may live their lives in a perpetual state of fear, doubting they can survive independently or without someone's help. Their behaviors can often elicit care-giving responses in others where they will give up their control or on the flip side, try to over-control their environment.

Individuals who have dependency as a core issue may appear clingy. Pessimism and self-doubt plague their lives. They may avoid making decisions, taking on responsibility, or having initiative. Life seems insurmountable to them. Being alone leaves them feeling anxious and vulnerable. Criticism or disapproval of any kind only reinforces their feelings of worthlessness.

Dependency is different from being codependent. Codependent people are not dependent on others but tend to attract people into their lives who depend on them. We will delve into the concept of codependency in more depth a little later on.

Entitlement

Individuals who have entitlement as a negative core belief see themselves as unique or superior and entitled to exclusive rights and privileges. Because they are exceptional, it only makes sense that they would also deserve a great deal of attention or praise from those around them. From this grandiose position, they may make demands or engage in behaviors without regard to how it may affect others. People who operate based on this core belief are the narcissists of the world.

They believe that they can do what they want, which can include rule-breaking. They are also not required, especially in their own minds, to reciprocate in social interactions, which can lead to resentment in others. People who develop this core belief use it to compensate for feelings of defectiveness or undesirability.

Unresolved core beliefs can significantly impact our relationships. When our needs as children are not met, we can develop a subconscious fear that our needs will never be satisfied. This early life trauma can cause us to base our relationship on need instead of love. A relationship built on need is a relationship based on fear. This often overlooked concept is why so many people end up settling for people they do not love or at times, even like. Their need to be in a relationship outweighs their need for happiness.

Whether they fear abandonment, rejection, or have other significant inner wounding, the bottom line is that they do not want to experience life on their own and will utilize whatever means possible to avoid it. Confusion may arise for the partner or spouse of these individuals because they may have a hard time discerning if they are actually loved or if they are only needed to satisfy the other's desperate attempts at feeling safe.

Are limiting beliefs controlling your life?
If so, which ones and why?

Defense / Coping Mechanisms

Defense mechanisms, also called personality defenses, are habitual internalized ways we manage our anxiety and cope with distressing emotions. Defense mechanisms keep us safe. They are an unconscious protective measure that, when triggered, help us defuse stressful situations. They develop in response to difficult or painful circumstances and work to protect us when we feel threatened. Most defense mechanisms are used unconsciously, meaning they are not under our mindful control.

All personality defenses succeed in helping people manage upsetting emotions. Some work better than others. There is a relationship between the type of coping mechanisms we use and our emotional maturity. People who are less emotionally mature will utilize primitive coping methods, while more emotionally mature individuals will lean towards more sophisticated ones. Primitive coping methods are reactive, not premeditative, in nature, and are typically an ineffective way of dealing with stress. Mature defense mechanisms are used deliberately and are employed consciously.

It is essential to know what defense mechanisms you employ, mainly if you primarily utilize less mature ones. It makes it easier to recognize and change our unconscious reactions into healthier, more mature ones when you do.

Primitive Defense Mechanisms

Primitive defenses are coping strategies that develop during early childhood. They are reactive and are triggered by our emotions as a way of avoiding short term pain. As an adult, primitive coping methods can cause more problems than they hope to solve. They may have served an essential function as we endeavored to survive our toxic upbringing, but they can interfere with healthy adult relationships.

Dissociation

We all dissociate at one time or another. How many times have you driven your car to a location and not have a conscious recollection of how you got there? You dissociated in these instances. You, as spirit, were out of your body and not in the present moment. On some levels, people who dissociate are not in touch with reality.

Dissociation, as a defense mechanism, is a strategy that is often used when fighting or fleeing (running away) is not an option. Our only choice is to shut down or "freeze" and "play dead" by leaving our bodies mentally and emotionally. It allows the triggered individual to disconnect from the real world, if only for a short time.

Projection

Projection is the inability to distinguish between the self and others. It is a break in reality, where the person inaccurately identifies the feelings they are experiencing as coming from someone else. This reaction is especially true if what they are feeling is anxiety-provoking and deemed unacceptable to express. This coping mechanism keeps us from dealing with or recognizing our real inner emotions and motivations. People who continuously use projection as a defense mechanism may have heightened levels of paranoia.

Acting Out

Many times people act out when they are unable to connect with, articulate, or express their feelings. They may throw a book, punch a wall, or slam a door instead. Acting out is an impulsive response used to relieve internal pressure and often helps the individual feel calmer and more peaceful afterward. Explosive tempers, any form of physical abuse, and even self-mutilation are all forms of acting out.

Denial

Denial is the most famous and well-known defense mechanism we may use. When someone is in denial, they refuse to accept reality or facts. A classic example of denial is when an alcoholic rejects the notion they may have a drinking problem. Denial protects us from having to deal with the pain and perhaps consequences associated with our life choices.

More Mature Defense Mechanisms

More mature defense mechanisms are a step up from the primitive defense mechanisms we have just discussed. Many adults employ these coping strategies. While they work, they are not ideal.

Repression

People who use repression as a defense mechanism tend to bury their painful, traumatic, or disturbing thoughts in their subconscious. Repression keeps the distressing experience from entering into their conscious awareness. Individuals use it as a means to avoid information that triggers anxiety. Survivors of sexual abuse often report the recovery of repressed memories years after the assault occurred. Repression is different from denial. When someone represses a thought, emotion, or experience, he or she forgets it versus merely refusing to accept it.

Displacement

When something frustrates or otherwise upsets us, someone who uses displacement as a defense mechanism will take their distressing feelings out on someone or something else. Many times this coping mechanism is tied to an inability to express our emotions to the person to whom they are intended in a safe way. This inner conundrum allows the individual to move from a place of inner powerlessness into a position in which he or she can feel like they are in control. This strategy may allow the person to vent his or her unsettled emotions, but the net result is that they end up hurting someone altogether innocent and unaware of what is going on.

Intellectualization

A person might employ intellectualization to distance himself or herself from an impulse, event, or behavior rather than deal with the painful or anxiety-producing emotions associated with it. Intellectualization occurs when we analyze a situation. It insulates and buffers a person from their feelings. Intellectualization is similar to rationalization.

Rationalization

Rationalization occurs when we try to explain away the bad behavior of ourselves or others. Enablers often use rationalization as a way of coping with the actions of an abuser.

They might contend that their spouse did not mean to hit them, but they had a bad day at work. For some, it allows them to pass on the blame. For others, it enables them to justify poor behavior. People who use this defense mechanism may also shift the focus of an event, put a different spin on it, or offer an alternative explanation of it.

Regression

People who use regression as a coping strategy revert to an earlier level of emotional development. Their behavior, in times of stress, can become childish, where they stomp off and slam the door. If you have ever experienced an adult having a temper tantrum, they have most likely regressed.

Mature Defense Mechanisms

People who have mature defense mechanisms have a stable connection to and understanding of reality. They are the most effective, adaptive coping mechanism and are the least responsive. Mature defense mechanisms, unlike the strategies explored earlier, work to correct the underlying problem instead of just ignoring them. They are something that anyone can use but require practice for them to overrule any earlier, more responsive defense mechanisms already in place.

Sublimation

Sublimation occurs when people consciously redirect energy and attention away from unacceptable thoughts or impulses into more acceptable outlets. By refocusing the mind, the person can channel their energy into something more productive. Rigorous exercise, the use of affirmations, and even humor can take our thoughts off a negative situation and help to discharge stress and anxiety.

Assertiveness

People who use assertiveness as a defense mechanism use their words in order to have their needs met in a direct, firm but respectful way. Assertiveness is an excellent strategy to use for people who tend to be either more aggressive or passive in their communication skills.

Passive people tend to be good listeners but often do not speak up for themselves. Aggressive people may be good leaders, but they are unable to listen to the wants and needs of others. People who use assertiveness as a coping mechanism, fall somewhere in the middle of the two. They can speak their mind in a courteous yet firm manner, but also can listen to and hear what others say to them.

Make a list of the defense mechanisms you use in order from most used to least. What does this tell you?

Family Roles

Living with an abuser can cause the family unit to work hard in an attempt to adapt to the changing uncertainty and ongoing craziness within the household. A variety of systems are adopted, each designed to reduce the stress within the home. One of these is the taking on of "family roles." Family roles are a series of recurring behavioral patterns children adopt to balance out and survive dysfunctional family systems.

Children play a critical role in attempting to establish and maintain a sense of peace and harmony within the home. In this effort, they will often take on, without realizing it, one of five roles. Some roles are more passive, while others are more active or aggressive. Some children assume their assigned role their entire lives, or it may be passed on from one family member to another when the original role keeper matures and moves out. Only children may play all of the rolls at one time in their lives or another. These roles consist of the Caretaker or Enabler, the Hero or Golden Child, the Scapegoat or Problem Child, The Mascot, and the Lost Child.

The Caretaker

The Caretaker, many times identified as the enabler, is the person who assumes responsibility for the happiness of the whole family. This position can be the spouse, though, in many family systems, this role often lands squarely on the oldest child. This child is thrust into the role of parent, assuming responsibility for younger siblings. Subsequent children naturally look to the Caretaker for safety and stability.

Children in the Caretaker role feel like they have to be responsible for what is going on around them. They are the fixers of the family and often believe it is their job to keep the family going. They may take the blame as a way to shield their brothers and sisters from being punished or experiencing other negative consequences. They are forced to take on a mature role at the expense of their own childhood and their own happiness. Caretaker children often feel like martyrs, and this may lead to feelings of resentment and bitterness.

The Hero

The Hero or Golden Child will do everything in his or her power to maintain the family's appearance. They may pretend everything is fine and that the family is good, normal, and healthy, all in an effort to save face. They may be overly responsible and self-sufficient, similar to the Caretaker.

These individuals seek achievement and success as a means to set themselves apart from the appearance of family dysfunction. It is common for the Hero to be involved in numerous activities. Their need for perfection, along with their intense drive, may leave them with high-stress levels or stress-related injuries. In many families, the Hero is the recognized "good" or "favorite" child and receives all the blessings associated with it.

The Scapegoat

The scapegoat is the problem child. They are traditionally viewed as being defective and are the ones blamed or held responsible for creating all of the family's issues. Unlike the Hero who pretends that everything is alright, the Scapegoat does the opposite — the Scapegoat rebels. Defiant and hostile, the Scapegoat may garner a lot of attention in the family, but it is always negative. These ambivalent children distract attention from what the real problem is: the parent's bad behavior.

Scapegoat children are typically the most sensitive and caring in the family and are often empathic. This sensitivity will often cause them to act out the ongoing tension within the household unknowingly. They are the "bad boy" or "bad girl" in a family. They may have problems in school, start using drugs, get pregnant, or even get in trouble with the law.

Their rebellious nature may also bring upon them the full wrath of the dysfunctional parent who will dole out additional or harsher punishment to better control or break these children. Scapegoat children are most often the first to leave home or the first to go into a recovery program.

The Mascot

The Mascot uses humor in an attempt to lessen the stress in volatile situations. Like the class-clown, the Mascot may crack jokes, perform antics, or employ some form of comedy to alleviate stress. It is their most defining characteristic. They use their sense of humor to deal with fear, pain, or anything that might cause emotional trouble.

Many times, the Mascot feels powerless to change anything that is going on around them. As an adult, they may have issues with responsibility. They may use their humor and silliness as a way to avoid serious duties and tasks as well as to mask their deep-seated insecurities. Many times the Mascot is a younger family member. This family placement does not require them to contribute in the same way older siblings do, but they are loved and protected by other family members.

The Lost Child

The Lost Child escapes the family drama by making themselves very small. They attempt to stay out of the way of family problems by being quiet and flying under the radar. The Lost Child tries to disappear and avoid interactions. They make few demands, never rebel, and never rock the boat all in an attempt to avoid notice. Instead, they spend a lot of time on their own and may withdraw into their own world. This characteristic is their way of dealing with reality. For them, this is the safest place to be. They just want a quiet life free of chaos.

The Lost Child often feels ostracized and inadequate. Many times, they assume that there is something wrong with them. If they were somehow better, then they would receive the love and affection they so desperately desire. Since the Lost Child rarely gets into trouble, he or she, like the Hero, improves the visibility of the family by supporting the concept that things in the family are all right.

Your emotional scars are more than likely affecting you today. Having a better understanding of what happened to you in your formative years offers you the opportunity to take a step back and make changes. You might not have had a choice when you were a child, but now you do. When we choose to look at ourselves, our history, our life patterns and decide to make changes to the core of our being, we can begin the process of breaking free of chronic cycles of dysfunction.

What was your family role?
What impact did it have as your life progressed?

Beyond The Physical Body

In western society, humanity's view of our existence on Earth is based solely on our interaction with the physical plane, where we live in a 3-dimensional world. We are all familiar with our physical bodies. We have two arms and legs, a head, torso, fingers, and toes. We are also made up of a heart and lungs, a liver and pancreas, hormones, peptides, and neurons. The physical body and the physical world only represent only one dimension of the human experience and embody only a fraction of the reality of the universe.

From this multidimensional viewpoint, each of us are made up of unseen energetic structures that are essential to life. They include the aura and subtle bodies, the chakras, the nadis, and our animating life force energy often referred to as "chi." The working of our subtle self plays a critical role in how we act and react to situations in our lives.

It is not my intention to write an in-depth thesis about metaphysical and New Age topics, but as we delve into further discussions about ourselves and our interactions with others, a base understanding of how we function on energetic levels is required. These insights will afford you another level of knowledge, another perspective of who you are and what is going on inside of you. It will also provide you a fresh look at your interactions with others. The views being presented here, although condensed, will support more advanced concepts disclosed later on in this text.

If this perception of the world is foreign to you, then welcome to the realm of subtle energy. Thousands of books and articles explore this topic, including my book *Avoiding The Cosmic 2x4*. Mainstream science overlooks the field of subtle energy, but its importance and role in our lives are tremendous. The intrinsic wholeness of a person cannot be considered apart from his or her totality, and this includes how our subtle energy system affects our physical, mental, and emotional wellbeing. We will start by exploring each of the elements that make up our energetic selves.

The Aura And Subtle Bodies

Surrounding our physical bodies is a field of subtle energy referred to in esoteric literature as the aura or auric field. It is our personal space. We recognize our personal space most acutely when someone infringes on it. When someone uninvitingly stands too close to us, we often experience a strange sense of physical discomfort. We may feel violated and wish they would take a step back. We can sense them and their energy even though physical contact has not occurred.

The aura is composed of a series of subtle bodies, the etheric body, the emotional or astral body, the mental body, and the causal body. Each subtle body has unique properties and plays a distinct role in our interactions with the world. Each subtle body vibrates at a different rate or frequency. The etheric body vibrates at the slowest frequency, although faster than the gross, denseness of the physical body, while the causal body vibrates at the highest rate. Each contains "*chakras*" or energy centers. The chakras connect to one another via the "*nadis*" or energy channels.

Everything that we think or do affects our auric field. It is also affected by the energies of our environment. It is our first line of defense. Our aura stands firm when the vibration of joy and love fill our inner world. It can effectively protect us from the invading energies of others. If we are scared, worried, or filled with dread, the vibration of our aura weakens. It becomes more porous. External forces can more readily influence us. Low vibrations of the auric field can leave us vulnerable, which can ultimately affect our wellbeing.

The Causal Body

The causal body is the world of spirit and pure energy. It represents the part of us that is closest to source or God. It is the first energetic construct that separates us as an individual from the world around us. It is the shell around which all of the other bodies form. Concepts such as "I" and "I am" are associated with this energy body. The causal body is involved with the creation of abstract ideas and concepts. It works to guide us to health, harmony, and wholeness.

The Mental Body

The mental body is the world of thought and concrete ideas. It reflects our ability to think and construct mental images. It is where our ideas transition from the nothingness of the causal body and enters into the constructs of the mind. It represents the energy of our thoughts, beliefs, and values. Thinking, imagery, perceptions, judgments, creativity, invention, and inspiration are all expressions of the mental body. It represents a projection of our inner reality that is conveyed out into the world.

The Emotional Or Astral Body

The astral or emotional body vibrates at a lower frequency than the mental body. Our feelings shape it, and it expresses itself through our emotions. It stores all of our emotions, including our inner wounding. Challenging situations can trigger inappropriate emotional responses and the associated coping mechanisms if these hurtful experiences are left unhealed. A reaction can occur regardless of if we have a memory of a past offense or not.

The emotional body unites the body and mind and provides integrity between our inner world and our outer experience. Our emotions activate or give energy to thoughts, which are formed and held in the mental body, into a vibration that can be experienced by the physical body.

The Etheric Body

The etheric body vibrates at a frequency closest to the physical body. The etheric body is concerned with the processes and activities of energy, in and around the physical body. It acts as the blueprint of the physical body, providing it with a framework or pattern upon which it is shaped and anchored. This non-physical body has the same characteristics as the physical body, such as organs, glands, and other anatomical features, but these structures exist outside of our normal perceptual range. It is said to supply information to the cells of our body, where it guides the physical body through its automated processes such as growth and development, repair, and healing.

The Chakras

The term chakra is a Sanskrit word that means wheel or disk. They can be thought of as spinning vortexes of energy within the subtle body. Each chakra acts as a receptor, transformer, and assimilator of energy. These energy centers process and store information from events that have affected us throughout our lifetime. It is through the chakras that we experience the world. Each subtle body contains seven major chakras, that line up in a vertical column up and down the spine. They are numbered one through seven. The first chakra resides at the base of the spine. The seventh chakra sits on the top of the head.

The First Chakra

The first chakra is located at the base of the spine and relates all things that are solid, earthy, and grounded. It is the center of manifestation into the physical world. On physiological levels, the first chakra controls the adrenal glands, the coccyx, and the coccyglelganglion as well as the large intestines. When we fear for our survival or feel threatened, our first chakra is triggered where it activates our fight or flight response. It is from the first chakra that we can ground ourselves, our physical body, as well as our subtle bodies via a grounding cord.

The Second Chakra

Moving up the body, the next energy center we come to, located between the navel and the genitals, is the second chakra. It acts as a controlling agent that "gives birth" to our creations upon the physical plane. Physiologically speaking, the second chakra is associated with the sacral vertebrae and the sacral plexus nerve ganglion. It is furthermore linked to the reproductive organs and in particular, the ovaries and testes. The second chakra is the interface between the world of energy and the physical world. It supports activities such as integration, creativity, and is the seat of our desires. It also controls our ability to recognize energy on feeling levels. This ability is called clairsentience.

The Third Chakra

There is only one word to describe the energetic nature of the third chakra: power. In the solar plexus, just below the sternum, is where the third chakra resides. Physiologically, this energy center is associated with the solar nerve plexus, the adrenal glands and the organs of digestion, where our bodies convert matter into energy.

The function of the third chakra is to produce and provide energy and power to all of our endeavors. It is the fire of combustion and is responsible for all movement and activity that leads to manifestation on the physical plane.

Accomplishment and completion of goals is a critical function of the third chakra. Without an initiating or propelling force, we would be unable to get our energetic motor running and manifest into the physical plane. The third chakra is critical in our ability to use our will and willpower. Will and willpower describe how we use our energy for ourselves, as in meeting our needs, as well as how we utilize our power when relating to others.

The Fourth Chakra

The fourth chakra vibrates at the energy of compassion, balance, and harmony. When we are in the energetic vibration of the fourth chakra, we can evaluate the goals we have established and reflect on our achievements. Located in the center of the chest, many call this energy center the "heart chakra" or "heart center". The thymus gland and the heart plexus are controlled by it.

The fourth chakra acts as an integrator or synthesizer of energies within each subtle body. We experience this as a sense of inner wholeness where our bodies and mind are one. We feel one with ourselves, congruent. We experience wholeness when the different aspects of our inner world are in harmony with one another. It leaves us feeling a sense of integrity with ourselves and the world. It is from this central point that all life radiates, connecting all of our parts. This center is a reflection of our wants, needs, desires, and ourselves. It is where we can tap into our sincerest wishes, hopes, and dreams. It is where we can connect with our souls.

The Fifth Chakra

Located in the cleft of the throat is the fifth chakra. Based on its physical location alone, it is no wonder that this chakra vibrates with the energy of communication. It controls our ability to express our thoughts, ideas, feelings, and emotions. On physiological levels, it is related to the cervical ganglia medulla as well as with the thyroid gland.

The fifth chakra houses our beliefs and belief systems. Our perception about ourselves, an event or situation can play a significant role in our ability to communicate. The fifth chakra allows us to transform our thoughts, concerns, creative ideas, opinions, and even emotions into a set of symbols that we collectively understand. We then use these symbols to communicate, to share our experiences with others, be it through the spoken word, writing or art.

The Sixth Chakra

The primary mode of the sixth chakra is that of sight, insight, and imagination. Physiologically, the sixth chakra is associated with the hypothalamus/pituitary nerve plexus and the pineal gland. Many will recognize it as the "third eye" that sits in the center of the forehead. The sixth chakra controls how we see ourselves and our environment and houses our ability to receive and process subtle visual information, which is called clairvoyance.

The Seventh Chakra

The pineal gland, the cerebral cortex, and the central nervous system are all linked to the seventh chakra. The seventh chakra is the seat of wisdom and sits on the top of the head. It is the gate between all that is yet to manifest and the physical world. It is the point from which all things begin and to which, in the end, all things return. It is through the seventh chakra that we connect with God, our higher self, or cosmic consciousness. The ability tied to insights gained via the seventh chakra is called knowingness.

The Nadis

Environmental information is transported into and out of the body via energy channels called nadis. There are nadis attached to each side of the chakras. Nadis also connect one chakra to another and one subtle body to another. The nadis direct and transfer energetic vibrations through the subtle bodies and into the physical body.

How It All Works: Energy Flow and the Subtle Energy System

We are each filled with life-giving energy called chi, which fills and animates us. Everything in the universe is dependent on the invigorating power this neutral energy provides, including ourselves. We experience it through its actions, even though it is unseen. It is generally agreed upon that, if deprived of this animating force, we would cease to exist. The structures of the subtle body support the movement of subtle energy, just like our arteries, veins, and capillaries support the flow of blood through the physical body.

The seven major chakras connect to each other via a vertical column of energetic matter that runs up and down the spine, which, according to Yogic traditions, is called the Sushumna. The Sushumna's function is to transport energy (chi) through the chakras. Whereas a nadi is like an electrical wire or a nerve that runs through our body, the Sushumna can is like a major electrical power bus. It functions like our spinal cord, which acts as an electrical highway for nerve transmission.

Through a nadi that extends upward out the seventh chakra, subtle energy comes into the body from "source." It is then transported through the Sushumna to the first chakra at the base of our spines. Energy exits the Sushumna through a downward-facing nadi that extends out of our first chakra, our grounding cord. This energy is then dispersed or "grounded" deep into the Earth.

The flow of energy through the Sushumna functions like a DC or direct current circuit. A DC circuit is an unbroken path through which an electric current flows from positive to negative. Electricity moves from a power source, such as a battery, to an output, or ground, where excess electricity is dissipated. An electrical current flows when a circuit is complete. The light bulb turns on. If the connection is somehow inhibited or faulty, the current cannot flow properly.

Likewise, if the circuit that makes up the Sushumna breaks, the flow of energy through the chakras stops or slows down. This breakdown of energy movement can happen if energy coming in via the seventh chakra is distorted or if the body, at the first chakra, is not grounded. This dynamic can cause numerous energetic concerns, such as not being grounded or causing us, as spirit, to be knocked out of our bodies and out of the present moment. (We will be coming back to this concept over and over again as we move forward.)

The nadis, that extend out in front of and behind the body, transport energy and information into and out of the remaining chakras. They do this by channeling data in from the world around us and through each subtle body.

Richard Gerber, author of *Vibrational Medicine: New Choices For Healing Ourselves*, likens the chakras to the functioning of electrical transformers. An electrical transformer reduces or amplifies the voltage of an electrical current. Chakras, like their physical counterparts, step down or increase subtle energy from one frequency to another. The chakras function as a sort of relay station where they slow down incoming energy until it reaches a vibration the subtle body can process. In essence, the chakras regulate the flow of energy into and out of our bodies, providing it to us in a form we can utilize.

The chakras of the mental body, for example, reduce the vibrational frequency of the energy it receives from the causal body. From here, it is either processed by the mental body or is passed on and slowed down even more as it travels to the lower vibrating subtle bodies. The flow of energetic information continues through each of our subtle bodies until it reaches the physical body, where a physiological or hormonal response occurs.

The Energy Of Thoughts & Emotions

Each of our thoughts, feelings, ideas, and emotions vibrate at a specific frequency, which we transmit to and receive from the world around us. Joy, for example, oscillates at one rate, while fear another. When we receive the vibration of joy from our environment, we interpret its vibrational pattern, on some level of our awareness, as joy. When we receive the energy of fear from the world around us, we likewise recognize it as fear.

Energetic vibrations travel in two directions, into us from our surroundings and out of us, back into the environment. Unseen vibrational information is continuously being transmitted or received by the chakras and nadis. It travels into the causal body and through each successive subtle body until it is ultimately manifest in the physical body as a physiological response. Correspondingly, our thoughts, feelings, ideas, and emotions, are transmitted through the subtle bodies and out into the world where it can be received and processed by others.

For example, when we are excited, enthusiastic, joyful, hurt, or upset, we transmit the vibration of these emotions through the subtle bodies, via the chakras and nadis, out into the world where we "tune" our surroundings. Once transmitted, the frequency of these emotions can be received by the chakras and nadis of others through their subtle bodies, ultimately creating a thought, a sensation, or biochemical response within them. This interplay of energetic non-verbal exchange forms the basis of healthy relationships and can underscore challenges in unhealthy ones.

According to John E. Nelson, the author of *Healing the Split*, at conception, we are all the way open to the flow of energy from our environment. He feels that at birth, one of the first things an infant does, as it learns to interact with the world, is to develop a sense of self. To do this, the infant forms what he calls a "psychic membrane" that allows it to filter information from the environment. All sensory information, he believes, undergoes this filtering process. This process occurs in the chakras.

Each chakra processes information within a specific band or range of frequency vibrations. They function similar to a typical AM/FM radio. You can listen to any FM station when you tune your set to the correct range. Let us say, for example, that your fourth chakra processes emotional information within the 88 to 108 MHz frequency range. One of the functions of the fourth chakra is to process the vibration of love, which in this instance, we will say vibrates at a frequency of 92.8 MHz.

If your fourth chakra is healthy, open, and functioning, you would be able to receive the frequency vibration of any station on the dial, including 92.8 MHz, the vibration of love. If there have been issues that have affected your fourth chakra, and your ability to experience love, your capacity to tune into it may be impaired.

We block the natural flow of energy moving through the chakras when we are in the midst of a traumatic event. Cringing is a great word to use when describing our energetic response to adversity. This reaction is normal and natural in the short term.

A history of unpleasant events throughout a lifetime can take a toll on our chakras' ability to function correctly. Chakras typically do not close all at once. They shut down gradually due to the repetition of hurtful or disturbing events. For example, we may find ourselves stuck in an unhealthy relationship, a job, or a habit. Over time, the chakras can become blocked, clogged, congested, or distorted and unable to process the information it receives correctly.

Going back to our love example, ongoing trauma may interfere with our ability to tune into the frequency of 92.8 MHz and our capacity to send or receive love. When we try to tune into this vibration, we may experience static. Given enough time, we may not be able to access this frequency vibration at all. The chakra is no longer cringing in response to a hurtful situation but is instead permanently braced for impact. The number of things that can adversely affect chakra functioning varies. Our core beliefs, the defense mechanisms we have chosen to employ, and or other response patterns we use when dealing with long-termed trauma play a significant role in chakra function.

This base explanation of our subtle self will serve as a foundation and provide us with a vocabulary to utilize as we delve into more advanced topics. We may not be able to see it, but we are all effected by subtle energy movement. If you have grown up in a household filled with abuse, then an understanding of the deeper levels of your being will help you to unravel what is going on inside of you and your psyche even further.

In The Moment

It is time to get back to our topic at hand. So far, we talked about the many shades of abuse, parenting and attachment styles, core beliefs, and family dynamics, each of which offered us the opportunity to know ourselves better. We have also looked at the coping mechanisms we may have employed when we were young to feel safe and make sense of our world. The net result is the consideration that these early life experiences may have influenced our now adult life. But how? How are they affecting us? Is there a signature or pattern that we can look for that might provide us with a sign that we are operating on archaic and dysfunctional programs?

Childhood abuse, as we have already described, can have long-lasting effects on an individual because of the traumatic stress it causes. The American Psychiatric Association defines a traumatic event as an experience that is threatening to the self or someone close to you, accompanied by intense fear, horror, or helplessness.

Dr. Robert Scaer, in his book *The Trauma Spectrum: Hidden Wounds and Human Resiliency*, states, "*the cumulative experiences of life's 'little traumas' shape virtually every single aspect of our existence.*" He suggests this accumulation of negative life experiences influences our unconscious feelings and life preferences, including our "*personality, choices of mate, profession, clothes, appetite, pet peeves, social behaviors, posture, and, most specifically, our state of physical and mental health and disease.*"

The maltreatment you experienced may have been chronic and prolonged, or it may have only occurred for a short period in your life. It may have been intense and overt or subtle and covert. Factors that contribute to our ability to maintain a sense of normalcy in our lives vary based on when the trauma occurred, its intensity, and the type encountered. Other factors that contribute to how someone fairs later on life can include a person's inner make-up and their innate sensitivity.

Did the child experience trauma early in life, or was it later when they were older and perhaps a bit more mature? Was their situation short-lived, or did it occur daily? With all of these factors and variables, it is impossible to say where on the trauma spectrum a survivor will fall, but fall they will.

The symptoms and associated behaviors of an adult survivor can become subtler as the individual learns to better cope with day to day life. Trauma survivors can often function well in several aspects of their lives. They may be able to talk about work or the weather, have high paying successful jobs, or be the president of the PTA. Then again, depending on their experiences and their reaction to them, they may be plagued by depression, anxiety, PTSD, anger, aggression, and substance abuse. If the trauma was early in life, long-lasting and severe, more encompassing mental health issues might be displayed.

Your subconscious mind, your subtle, and even your physical body can be triggered by a fearful experience that occurred many years earlier. Studies indicate that you do not have to have a memory about a past trauma to be affected by it. Interestingly, research shows that when a child grows up, he or she will utilize the same coping skills and defense mechanisms they did when they were young. They may also respond to challenges in their intimate relationships using the same attachment style they did as an infant. The net result is they might be doing great in many aspects of their lives, that is, until they encounter a situation that activates an unresolved emotional wound.

Emotional Triggers

We all have had negative experiences in our lives. When we find ourselves in a similar situation, the pain, fear, or other emotion we initially experienced can be stirred up, and we are "triggered." An emotional trigger is a reaction to an external event or circumstance that sets off a conscious or unconscious memory.

Triggers are automatic and involuntary and are a response to a perceived threat. A certain time of the year, a particular smell, the way someone touches you, or something they say, can subconsciously transport you back in time. The intense emotion often associated with our early wounding can activate our stress response mechanism and, depending on how we have learned to cope with life challenges, can set off symptoms of anxiety, panic, discouragement, despair, or negative self-talk.

Different things trigger different people. Triggers are very personal and can be activated long before the person realizes they are upset. One thing about triggers is that they always match some aspect of our traumatic life experiences.

Perhaps you are having an enjoyable conversation with an acquaintance. Then, out of the blue, your friend makes an off-handed comment. Without understanding why or what happened, you may feel your blood pressure rising, or your heart may start racing. Your body might tighten up. You may feel hurt, ashamed, or embarrassed. Their comment might anger you, or your internal negative self-talk may turn on. What just happened? You got triggered.

Many people struggle to cope with situations that remind them of a traumatic event. This phenomenon is especially true for children who suffered from abuse. Often we are not aware of what triggers us. The unconscious nature of triggers makes managing our reaction to what is going on challenging. We are subject to our emotions instead of being in control of them. There are innumerable things that can set us off. Below is a list of common triggers, but anything that pushes a button within us and provokes an automatic internal response IS a trigger.

Common Triggers

- Being cheated on.
- Being touched or having someone come on to you.
- Hurting or being in pain.
- Being scared.
- Hearing bad news.
- Being criticized.
- Feeling discounted, ignored or misunderstood.
- Feeling disrespected.
- Losing (such as losing a game).
- Feeling left out.
- Being interrupted.
- Having things not go as you planned.
- Feeling like you are unfairly treated.
- Being bossed around and told what to do.
- Feeling rejected or that a friend or loved one will leave you.
- Being judged, blamed, or shamed.
- Feeling like someone is trying to control you.
- Experiencing someone as needy or trying to smother you.
- Feel as if someone is not honoring you or your values.

The Present Moment

We are firmly planted in our bodies when we feel whole, confident, powerful, and secure. Our life force energy (chi) is flowing. In this state, we feel calm and relaxed, our anxiety is low or absent, and life's little difficulties have a hard time sticking to us.

When we are triggered, a number of things happen. First and foremost, we, as spirit, are knocked out of our subtle energy bodies. The quantity or quality of subtle energy that moves through our energy channels becomes impaired. Our ability to ground the body becomes diminished. This dynamic causes us to hold on to activated negative thoughts and emotions. These discordant vibrations can become trapped within us and create several adverse reactions, including having difficulties being in the present moment.

When we are not in the present moment, we miss out on life as it unfolds before us. We are not experiencing what is happening right here and right now. Granted, we all daydream and space out. Evidence suggests that daydreaming, creativity, and the imaginative mind often go together. It allows us to free-flow thoughts and ideas, which can lead to a eureka moment.

When we are triggered, we are not daydreaming. Triggering often brings on a cascade of thoughts that can keep us in a negative thought pattern and out of the present moment. Our thoughts are either in the past or in the future. We may not realize we have mentally digressed while in this state and may believe that we are utilizing our mental energy in a helpful, productive way. We may find ourselves trying to deal with situations by going over them again and again in our minds. When this occurs, we are experiencing something called "intrusive thoughts."

Intrusive Thoughts

It is normal to react emotionally to things that happen to us. If we are in good working order, a thought can come into our minds, our bodies may respond to it, but after a short time, we can let it go and move on with our lives. If you have a high emotional reaction to what occurred, your mind might want to keep the situation alive. This mental state typifies the realm of intrusive thoughts.

An unwanted and intrusive thought is a thought pattern that becomes stuck in your head. It is like hearing the lyrics to a song over and over again and cannot make it stop. These thoughts may revolve around work, our decisions, our relationships, our safety, our religious choices, or our sexual orientation. We can have intrusive thoughts on just about any topic if there is an emotional charge that activates a negative core belief within us. Worry and rumination are the most common forms of persistent negative thinking.

Rumination

Rumination is when we over-think or obsess over a situation that is upsetting to us. People will often ruminate when something frustrating, threatening, or insulting happens, such as at work or in one of our relationships. Our emotional wounds trigger these negative thought patterns.

If you are not sure what rumination is, you may experience it as a record or video that keeps playing in your mind. It is when you relive the details of an argument with a friend and just cannot let it go. Many times we do not even realize we are ruminating. Our mind keeps coming back to the same situation regardless of what we do to shake it off.

It is normal to want to process our emotions, learn from our experiences, or come up with an alternative solution. People who ruminate tend to get stuck in thought patterns that focus on concepts such as recent mistakes, missed opportunities, actions taken or not taken, losses, and personal slights. People who ruminate hope that, through their intense concentration, the outcome will somehow change or, if faced in a similar situation in the future, will turn out differently.

Rumination starts innocently. It is our mind's attempt to make sense of what just happened to us. Where rumination differs from problem-solving is that people who ruminate never get to the point of resolution but instead become trapped in their own emotions. The bad thing about rumination is that it often leaves us feeling worse off than better. It is the ultimate stress magnifier. It takes a situation in which we already feel anxious and amplifies it. Each time we think about the offending circumstance, we become upset all over again. We can ruminate for hours, days, or even weeks, that is, until we can break free of this mind-numbing cycle.

Rumination can be challenging to give up. Feelings of hopelessness and powerlessness fuel it. We can never change a situation that has already happened by going over and over it in our minds. We cannot deliver a witty comeback or better response to something that has already occurred, regardless of how hard or how much we think about it.

The Worry Cycle

Worry is a normal part of everyday life. Worrying is similar to rumination, where our minds can become trapped in an endless cycle of trying to figure things out. The critical difference between the two is that people who ruminate focus their mental energy on resolving past events, while worriers are focused on the future.

When we worry, we imagine potential outcomes for unknown or pending events. We use it in an attempt to solve suspected problems in our lives. We all have moments when we think about a situation at work, an issue in a relationship, or a potential health concern.

Worry does have some positive attributes, such as alerting us to potential crises. It can motivate us into creative problem-solving. It is when our thoughts become persistent and uncontrollable that they become a cause for concern.

Worry is a cycle of living with the question "what if" in the forefront. This internal mechanism can become an issue if worst-case scenario thinking is the only solution we have to our problems. Worry can be the first stage in a much larger negative thinking process. It often underscores the manifestation of its much more insidious forms: anxiety and panic, with worry on the mild side and a full-blown panic attack on the other.

Worry can become a concern if we are unable to ground and shake loose of the arousing thoughts, which, if given enough momentum, can interfere with our daily lives. It can quickly transform itself into anxiety when you add fear to the picture.

Fear

Fear is an unpleasant or disturbing feeling brought about by a perceived or real physical or emotional threat. We feel scared in anticipation of something terrible happening to us. Feeling fearful is designed to alert us to danger. This emotional response is ancient and is not just seen in humans but appears in animals as well. It causes, or better stated, precipitates a metabolic change in our bodies that influence organ function and personal behaviors. Animals, in a threatening situation, will run, hide, flee, or freeze when they perceive danger.

We all share a similar physiological response to fear in that it activates our fight or flight stress response. It was essential to early man's survival. In today's world, real life or death situations are rare. The reasons why we may respond to an event with fear is wide-ranging and highly personalized and far exceeds what we can recognize consciously.

We may fear rejection, loss, failure, disappointment, or making a mistake. We may be fearful of unexpected things happening to us or fear for our life or our health. We may fear the path society is taking just as much as we may fear spiders, heights, or snakes. Things that can trigger a fear response are endless. Regardless of the perceived threat, the brain and body still respond the same when activated. The addition of fear into the worry cycle can escalate our worry.

Anxiety

Anxiety is the expression of worry with a dash of fear thrown in for good measure. Anxiety, like fear, serves as an internal early warning sign of impending danger. We experience it as a body level feeling of uneasiness or discomfort.

Anxiety is like a one-two punch. The worry of our conscious or unconscious mind triggers a fear response, which in turn activates our fight or flight mechanism. Our fear response operates by providing us with short bursts of physiological changes, such as the release of survival hormones.

Many people experience anxiety for extended periods. We feel anxious as long as we are in a chronic worry cycle. Once we can break out of the thoughts of impending gloom and doom, our bodies can relax and let go of the activated fear. When this happens, our anxiety is naturally lessened.

Some researchers suggest that fear and anxiety are separate, but fear always underscores anxiety. People who suffer from chronic anxiety feel fatigued or suffer from adrenal burnout because their bodies are never able to rest. Their internal systems are always on guard and ready to go. It is not the anxiety that is keeping their systems revved up; it is the underlying fear.

Panic

Take anxiety (worry and fear) and put it on overdrive, now you have panic. We experience panic when the body and mind feel overwhelmed. We can panic when we are in an immediate life-threatening situation. Still, there are countless people who experience panic, in the context of a panic attack, who are not responding to an impending threat.

A panic attack can come on suddenly and is an episode of an intense, overwhelming feeling of fear tied to overstated physical reactions. The moderate physical sensations experienced when someone is anxious dramatically increase and can include a racing heartbeat, shortness of breath, trembling, chest pain, sweating, and nausea. People who suffer from panic attacks often feel like they are losing control or, even worse, may be dying.

The Energetics Of The Worry Cycle

The worry cycle worry takes on particular characteristics when looked at via the movement of life force energy through the subtle body. The cycle first emerges in the mental body with the appearance of worry. Worry, in and of itself, is a thought and may enter our internal space as an image of a potential situation. By themselves, they do not elicit emotional responses.

We can be cut off in traffic one day, and we might respond to the rude driver by courteously braking and continuing our travels unaffected. We can have a similar situation happen on a different day. Instead of remaining calm, cool, and collected, the event can trigger something in us. We may find ourselves laying on the horn at the discourteous individual, cursing the day they were born.

The worry cycle follows the same pattern. There might be something going on in our lives that may cause us to worry, but that moment quickly passes. If, on the other hand, something within us gets triggered, we may find ourselves moving further along into the worry cycle.

Enter fear. Where worry sits in the mental body, the world of thought, fear resides in the emotional body. The emotional body acts as a bridge between the mental and physical body. When activated, it takes the thoughts, beliefs, ideas, and judgments, of the mental body, and transmutes them into a form that can be felt physically. If you have unhealed wounds (which also reside in this layer), fear can activate them, sending ripples from your emotional body further down your subtle energy system into your etheric body.

The etheric body is what provides the final form to all things that manifest in the physical body. Medical intuitives can often find the vibration of health concerns in the etheric body on the brink of breaking through into physical symptoms. Chronic anxiety resides primarily in the etheric body. Its pattern sits in the background and keeps the adrenal glands on high alert, waiting for a potential disaster.

When we have a thought, and our emotions are activated, our emotions become the precursors of physiologic responses in the etheric body. If an intense and sufficient enough trigger is activated, the flow of energy continues, and we have a physiological response. Depending on what is going on, what is being triggered, the amount or type of inner wounding tied to it; the etheric body will manage how significant the physiological response will be.

Fear, as an emotional energy, is also tied to the first chakra. The first chakra supports the safety of our physical bodies and is critical to the activation of our fight or flight stress response. Our first chakra constricts when fear enters the picture. The energy of our worry has no place to go when this happens. We are unable to or may have problems letting our worries continue its travel down our grounding cords and out of our bodies. A contracted first chakra always causes the energy of our worries to loop around inside of us, creating the incessant and intrusive thought patterns. This energy dynamic, of a compromised first chakra, is also found in individuals who ruminate.

When someone has a panic attack, it is as if all hell has broken loose within our energy system. Increased amounts of stress hormones are released, and the body reacts accordingly. For people who are prone to panic attacks, a maladaptive pattern in the etheric body makes it easier for the body to respond in an undesired and reflexive way.

Triggers knock you out of the present moment and can put you into a cycle of worry or rumination. It is impossible to begin making changes and disarming the things that are activating your inner wounds if you do not even know they exist or that they are affecting you. Later in this text, we will address a series of concepts that will help you move out of these negative thought cycles and into happy, positive ones.

The Empath & Narcissist

We have all been brought up with the notion of vampires. We can easily imagine Count Dracula, in his long black cape, suckling the neck of a hapless victim. Stories of vampires fill the silver screen. Dracula, Son of Dracula, Blacula, Nosferatu, Twilight, Interview With A Vampire, and Blade are movies all based upon Bram Stoker's classic portrayal of Dracula. The life of Vlad the Impaler, the Transylvanian born 15th-century prince of Wallachia, inspired Stoker's bloodsucking, shape-shifting, immortal villain Dracula.

These creatures of the night, to sustain their vitality, are purported to feast on human blood. Vampires, as seen in the movies, may only be a fictitious character. There are, unfortunately, real-life living breathing vampiric individuals. You may have already encountered one. These leechlike creatures are energy vampires.

Energy vampires create a parasitic relationship between themselves and others. They intentionally, or more often unintentionally, feed off the life force energy of unsuspecting individuals instead of consuming their blood. Energy vampires are unable to sustain their chi at healthy levels. Their ability to produce this vitalizing energy is depressed or not functioning correctly. They look towards others to support their depleted resources, thus boosting their own. These energy-sucking individuals could be your parents, coworkers, husbands, wives, or friends.

An individual may become an energy vampire because they were violated or traumatized as a child, making it difficult for them to connect with this part of their being. They may discover at an early age how to siphon their shortage of energy off others. Energy vampires can also learn these negative traits if they grew up in an environment where their parents stole the lifeblood from them or others.

An energy vampire does not have long pointed teeth or wear a black cape. Most energy vampires are undetectable upon first glance. They often appear as well-meaning ordinary people. It is only when you spend a little time with one that they reveal their true colors.

The goal of an energy vampire is to control you and your energy. They use a variety of ways to influence you that fall into two major categories - extroverted and introverted. The extroverted energy vampire will seem highly attractive. You might find yourself mysteriously fascinated by them. They may have a strong opinion about themselves, their ideas, and their beliefs. In a more negative light, their self-serving outgoing nature may cause them to be stubborn, opinionated, or angry. Think about the drama queen who can stir up the energy in a room in a single bound. Energy vampire!

Introverted energy vampires, on the other hand, take on a very different form. They may complain incessantly about their problems, giving you little, if any, opportunity to respond or interact. They may throw pity parties or have a "poor me" attitude towards life – the consummate victim.

Both types of energy consumers are typically self-centered and self-absorbed. They may use guilt, fear, anger, sadness, or a variety of emotions to manipulate you. They will feed off of the positive vibes you emit but are also known to nourish themselves off negative emotions as well. They will pick fights, cause unnecessary problems, or invent imaginary illnesses all in an attempt to get a reaction from you.

When the concept of an energy vampire is taken to the furthest extent, enter the narcissists and psychopaths of the world who are known for bleeding you dry. They fill their gullet with "narcissistic supply," meaning the life force energy that you, the victim, provide.

Believe it or not, it is not all one-sided when talking about energy vampires. There is a consistent energy dynamic that occurs between the energy vampire and its food source - the host. The host is an individual whose life force an energy vampire is draining. Some children learn early on how to provide their life force energy to others, making them excellent hosts. Their training incorporates how to remain quiet and passive, regardless of what is going on around them. Their submission allows energy vampires to recharge their batteries and boost their depleted energy supplies, many times without the host understanding what is happening to them.

Surprisingly, and as weird as this may sound, the host does get something in return that keeps him or her giving their energy away. The interactions they have might leave them feeling loved, needed, valued, or in some cases, safe. Some even find their exchanges with an energy vampire satisfying or believe that they are fulfilling their life purpose. Regardless of the reward, their core beliefs will keep them lined up to give more.

Energy vampires steal vitality from their victims by upsetting their auric field. The vampire achieves this through one of his or her well-practiced introverted or extroverted manipulation tactics. Their first maneuver is to interfere with your grounding, which will knock you out of the present moment. Your mind will begin to wander, and you will start to become unaware of what is going on around you. You may find yourself ruminating over their strange behavior, the cruel things they say, or their blatant disrespect for all you stand for. In these moments, you might find yourself spending all of your mental energy trying to figure out what just happened or what is going on in general.

The spaced out, not in the present moment state you are in, leaves the door wide open for the energy vampire to invade. Your whole body can react when an energy vampire is feeding off of you. Your heart or gut may tighten because, on some level, your body recognizes something is wrong. You may find yourself feeling tired, bored, hopeless, lacking motivation, becoming irritated, overwhelmed, disoriented, depressed, or feel out of sorts. How you respond to these individuals may also seem odd and out of character.

Everything changes once your encounter with an energy vampire concludes. Your energy space has a chance to readjust, and you can once again return to the present moment. You will almost immediately notice that you feel happier, lighter, and more energetic with renewed inner strength and greater clarity when out of their sphere of influence. That is until you run into them once more. Then the process can start all over again.

Energy vampires, unlike their movie counterparts, are real. Their need to feed off your life force energy is real, as well. Their negative behavior compromises you each time you interact with one. Their tactics for knocking you out of the present moment robs you of your choices and interferes with your ability to live a happy, self-directed life.

Are you the victim of an energy vampire?

Now that we have had the opportunity to explore the concept of individuals who exhibit a parasitic nature, and their willing victims, we are going to take this concept to the next level. We will be utilizing words such as empath to describe the host and narcissist to identify the worst kind of energy vampire. A distinct relationship forms between these two types of individuals. It is like a well-choreographed dance that takes place once they meet and connect. These two personality types, when combined, can only lead to unhappiness, at least for the host.

The Creation Of Empaths And Narcissists

Much time and energy, in scientific circles, has been spent studying the development of the narcissistic personality. In contrast, aside from a handful of authors, little time has been devoted to exploring how empaths and other highly sensitive people came into being.

According to author, and intuitive psychiatrist Judith Orloff, MD, there are three primary reasons why an individual may become an empath. Orloff suggests that some babies are born this way. They naturally come into the world more sensitive. Others, she speculates, receive this gift as part of their genetic inheritance. These highly sensitive children come from a family where the parents and perhaps grandparents are also sensitives. This trait can be nurtured and developed, where the child is taught to recognize and honor their inborn gift. The third reason she proposes is that individuals become empaths because of early life trauma.

In a recent Facebook survey of individuals who identify themselves as empaths, over 80% of the 1,300 respondents reported some form of abuse or neglect during their formative years. This finding indicates that the vast majority of empaths become hypersensitive to their environment as a direct result of early life trauma.

Similarly, there are several theories about why individuals become narcissists. These children, like the empath, may the byproduct of a narcissistic parent who taught them the tips and tricks of narcissism. It may develop because the parent(s) have poor boundary function. These parents, in pursuance of their own self-care, tend to say yes to their child's every whim to keep the peace. These children never learn limits or how to cope with disappointment.

The majority of contemporary researchers into the most severe cases of narcissism suggest that narcissism forms as a way of compensating for feelings of defectiveness. These soon to be narcissistic children, like the empath, come into the world sensitive. They also experience significant wounding and trauma early on. They may have suffered from severe abuse, neglect, or punishment. These children, because they are not getting the love, approval, and acceptance they desire, develop unhealthy and inappropriate ways of receiving it or as in the case of a narcissist, of taking it in any way they can.

Emotional wounding is the parallel life experience felt by the majority of empaths and narcissists. It may be hard to believe that two people, with such vastly different characteristics, could experience similar life circumstances. The difference between these two diametrically opposed personality types come down to how the child dealt with the trauma they experienced.

By-and-large, Empaths, and narcissists both enter into the world as highly sensitive individuals. They both grow up in toxic environments, a literal war zone, often in a constant state of fear. Their challenging situation forces the immature mind to find ways of coping with their circumstances. Both come out of the tunnel with a dysfunctional view of themselves, life and the world in general. They both may feel broken, worthless, undesirable, unlovable, or that there is something inherently wrong with them. They both may have suffered, physical, mental, or emotional abuse or experienced a life filled with parental neglect. The net result is that one, as we will explore further, opens themselves up, and the other shuts themselves down.

When a child does not receive the love, trust and acceptance they deserve, that sensitive, fragile self has to make a choice. They can accept what is going on and adjust to the reality they face, or they can change their reality in an attempt to protect themselves. Their ability to adapt is the primary difference between an empath and a narcissist. Said in another way; both the empath and narcissist got hurt when they were young. They both had similar experiences, but their journey forward has not been the same. One chose to grow from their experience, the other shut down.

Empaths deep within their souls long to be loved and accepted. They pray that one day their situation will change. Their longing to experience the nurturing they so desperately desire causes them to internalize, "*One day it will happen. Then the despair and sadness I have felt for so long will magically fade away.*"

Their inner hope and their innate ability to cope with what is going around them keep them connected to God, source, and higher energies. They allow their life force energy to flow into them via the seventh chakra and out their grounding cords. Their connection to source enables them to release their pain and inner turmoil on some levels and recover.

For many empaths, this ability to recapture their essence can play a significant role in an ongoing trap of abuse, where they, now that their inner world feels better, will go back for more. This repetitive pattern of going back is something they also learned early on.

A Baleen whale offers an excellent analogy to an empaths' inner behavior. Baleen whales include the Blue whale and the Humpback Whale. These toothless mammals of the sea, when feeding, will open their mouths wide and filter a school of krill or other types of animal plankton from the surrounding seas. Empaths, who grow up in a toxic environment, act similarly. They will open themselves up wide in anticipation of receiving some nourishment. Even the smallest amount of love or affection directed their way can provide them with enough sustenance to keep them going. The less nurturing they receive, the more empathic they can become.

Empaths also use this gift to detect subtle and slight changes in their environment. They do this to keep a finger on the pulse and temperament of those around them. Can their inner self come out and play, or do they need to run and hide? Their need to be aware, alert and on guard can lead to hypervigilance and increased intuitive abilities. In return, for a safe and stable environment, they will do whatever it takes to continue receiving something, anything. Many times, they will exhibit the Subjugation/People Pleasing core belief.

These children's openness, their dreams of deliverance from their tormentors, tied to dysfunctional coping mechanisms, can open the door to the calling in of non-corporeal beings, namely attached entities. Attached entities are the narcissists, the energy vampires of the spirit world. While this is not a topic we will be discussing within the pages of this book, it is a concept I cover in-depth in my book *Dark Angels: An Insider's Guide To Ghost, Spirits & Attached Entities*.

Narcissist children make different choices than empathic ones when dealing with adversity. They chose to shut down. Their wounds cause them to cut themselves off from source. This choice causes their emotional development to become stuck at the age of the major trauma. Instead of accepting the reality of what is going on around them, they opt for Plan B, where they change reality to suit their needs.

Narcissistic children often feel the same level of worthlessness or brokenness as the empath, but are unable to cope, or chose not to deal with their intense self-deprecating emotions. They are not able to connect to source, release their emotional energy, and recover from traumatic events but work to transmute their pain by projecting it out into the world. In essence, they lose hope and give up. In its place, they construct what is called the "false self," where reality becomes what they say it is. They convince themselves, and hopefully others, that the false self is, in fact, their real authentic self. The maintenance of the false self causes them to lie not only to those they encounter but to themselves.

Empaths and narcissists may come from the same mold, but the way they cope with life and life events are vastly different. In a strange twist of fate, it is common to find unhealed empaths and narcissists drawn to each other in an unhealthy relationship bond.

The Anatomy Of An Empath

Confusing as this may be, being an empath and having empathy is not the same thing. Empathy is the ability to experience another's thoughts and feelings from their point of view. When we have empathy, we can step inside someone else's shoes and relate to their experiences even if we have not had that same experience ourselves. It allows us to see things from a perspective outside of our own and understand and relate to the feelings the other individual is having.

The ability to be empathetic is an innate part of the human experience. If someone we know loses a child, a spouse, a job, or experiences other hardships in their lives, empathy allows us to relate to them from a heartfelt, compassionate place.

This ability falls onto a scale with some people being able to express more empathy than others. If empathy is on one side of the scale, individuals who suffer from Cluster B personality disorders such as histrionic, borderline, narcissistic, or antisocial personality disorder exist on the other. People who fall under Cluster B personality disorders tend to show little if any empathy at all.

An empath, on the other hand, experiences a friend's loss in a very different way. They will often feel what a friend is going through, except literally in their body. They may feel the same emotional pain, the sadness, or the anxiety as if he or she were the one going through the loss themself. Being an empath is often viewed as a blessing and a curse. By understanding our empathic nature, we will add another piece to the puzzle of who we are and how we tick.

Highly Sensitive People

We all feel sensitive at one time or another. We have all had a gut feeling about a person or situation. We may detect that something is just not right, even though there is no evidence, visually or otherwise, to prove it. Some people respond to external stimuli more intensely. In her book, *The Highly Sensitive Person,* Dr. Elaine Aron explores how people deal with external information, a phenomenon called "sensory processing".

Sensory processing, according to Aron does not refer to input received via the sense organs, but is *"an increased sensitivity of the central nervous system and a deeper cognitive processing of physical, social and emotional stimuli."* Thus, if a person responds to external stimuli on deeper levels, the individual is considered "highly sensitive." One in five people are considered highly sensitive.

Highly sensitive people are prone to arousal, especially after exposure to stressful physical, mental, emotional, and social stimuli. They tend to react to situations more intensely than less sensitive individuals do. Their nervous system is exceptionally receptive to detecting and reflecting other people's moods. They are often easily overstimulated by external stimuli, such as loud noises, bright lights, strong smells as well as chaotic environments. This overstimulation can set off a triad of inner processes, which at times can seem overwhelming and leave them feeling tired and worn out. On the plus side, their higher level of sensitivity offers them the ability to pick up on subtle changes within their environment.

Scientists have recently discovered a group of specialized cells in the brain which they call "mirror neurons." Accordingly, these cells are said to allow us to share the joy, pain, and fear of others. They conjecture outside events, such as observing people's actions, trigger these cells. They go on to contend that the mirror neuron system is involved in our ability to experience empathy. Highly sensitive individuals, they speculate, have hyper-responsive mirror neurons, while individuals who lack empathy have an under-active mirror neuron system.

Mirror neurons do not explain the range of emotions that highly sensitive individuals perceive, which puzzles scientists. Sadly, modern science fails to investigate the subtle nature of our being, how energy flows in from the world around us and affects us physiologically, including activating mirror neurons.

From an energetic perspective, highly sensitive people are more in tune with what is going on around them. Their chakras may be more open to receiving and processing information. Information may flow better through their subtle bodies and subtle energy system in comparison to less sensitive individuals. They may also be better trained or have more experience, in acknowledging (processing) the vibration of the energy they are receiving.

Empaths

People who are empaths take the concept of being highly sensitive to an even higher level. They can directly experience what someone else is feeling. They mirror a person's physical, mental, and emotional pain as if they were residing inside the other person's body. They are finely tuned instruments. They are hypersensitive to the inner state of others and can detect small changes in the emotional undercurrents that surround them.

Empaths do not require an external cue, such as a phone call, a look on someone's face, or another person's emotional reaction to detect something going on. Empaths tune into situations intuitively. Many times, all an empath has to do is think about someone (consciously or unconsciously) to know what they are experiencing. Physical contact or even being in the same location is not required.

Empaths are often psychic sponges. They can soak up the emotional energy others project and absorb it right into their bodies. They internalize the feelings and physical sensations of others, which at times, can be intense and overwhelming. This ability can make it hard for an empath to distinguish someone else's internal pain, for example, from their own. It is also difficult for an empath to differentiate between what they are feeling about a given situation from what they are taking on from others. Their emotions can readily get confused, comingled, distracted, or influenced by others. The unintentional taking on of emotional energy can lead to confusion because the empath many times cannot figure out why they feel the way they do.

In scientific circles, this transmission of information is called an "emotional contagion." An emotional contagion is defined as the phenomenon where an individual feels similar feelings to others. This transference of emotional energy can occur between two people or collectively in larger groups, such as the frenzy experienced when a riot breaks out. Accordingly, empaths are more prone to experiencing emotional contagions.

This view supposes that contagion transmission occurs via facial expressions, vocalizations, and other nonverbal cues, ones in which the brain unconsciously responds. The receiver, via the activity of their mirror neurons, automatically mimics what they observe. This theory, again, does not explain how empaths can tune into the emotions of individuals who are hundreds, if not thousands, of miles away and are devoid of any physical or vocal contact. Like our discussion of mirror neurons, the working of the subtle energy system in its ability to receive and process information from the environment does.

Emotional contagion or not, an empath's internal state can change at the speed of light. They might be happy in one moment and filled with dread in the next. It is not that they are in the midst of a situation that causes this dramatic change, but instead, they have encountered someone who is projecting this energy, and they have inadvertently picked it up.

The sensitive nature of an empath is not something you can decide to get rid of. Some people become very good at blocking it out while others chose to numb out what they are perceiving by resorting to drugs, alcohol, or other destructive addictive behaviors as a remedy.

People who are empaths often find themselves wanting to help other people. They are loving, caring, compassionate, selfless, natural caregivers, and great listeners. Strangers find it easy to bear their souls to an empath, often divulging their deepest and darkest secrets before they realize what they are doing. People are often attracted to them because of the warm, deep inner light they project. Many tend to find themselves in healing professions. Doctors, nurses, counselors are often careers filled by empaths, but any job in a healing role qualifies. Empaths are often truth-tellers, as well. Speaking anything but their inner truth feels instinctively wrong to them.

Adding to our empathy spectrum, we find empaths on the far left of the spectrum, highly sensitive people a little further to the right, people who have and experience empathy, somewhere in the middle, and again, individuals with Cluster B personality disorders on the far right.

Clinical Psychologist, Abdul Saad, further breaks down the empathic end of the spectrum, where he identifies three types of empaths, the Authentic Altruist, the Proud Helper, and the Co-dependent.

Authentic Altruist

The Authentic Altruist has a high degree of inner awareness and a good understanding of their internal motivations. This awareness provides them with the freedom to choose. They can decide if they want to give of themselves or not and are not attached to the outcome of a situation. They allow individuals to choose their own life path, where they can experience their own karma and make life corrections as necessary. It takes work, according to Saad, to get to this more enlighten place. Individuals who reach this stage are often on a spiritual path or a journey to inner self-discovery.

Proud Helper

Proud Helpers are kind and loving individuals. Challenges start to appear when their egos step in. They may try to help another person, but this support may come from a place of self-deception. Often, they believe they understand what the other person needs. "*Mama knows best.*" They may be doing it to get their own needs met. If their care and support is not coming from an altruistic place it can leave the Proud Helper feeling resentful, especially if their efforts are not appreciated or reciprocated.

Codependent

Co-dependent people have an obsessive need to fix, save, or heal someone. This desire can become overwhelming and obsessive. Core issues an empath carries can be triggered if they are not in some way paid back for all of the energy they expend helping others. This expression of their empathic nature is unhealthy. We will be discussing the concept of empaths, people-pleasing, and co-dependency in the next chapter.

People Pleasing: The Aversion To Displeasing

People-pleasing is a behavior that is supported by society in general. Women, in particular, learn early on that it is their responsibility to help other people experience contentment in their lives. At the same time, they should not expect anything in return. Many children from dysfunction families discover that responding to other people's needs ahead of their own is the best and often right thing to do. This belief in giving up of oneself is contradictory to someone who develops through the eyes of narcissist entitlement, a subject we will address shortly.

Empathic children who operate based on the subjugation/people-pleasing core belief quickly discover that to survive in their young world; the best and safest thing to do is to comply with their parents' wishes. Some resolve that this is what they have to do to win their parent's love and approval. Others realize this strategy helps to reduce conflict and avoid punishment. In either case, they learn early on to put up and shut up. In order to be a good boy or girl, it is best not to make waves.

Being agreeable to others in moderation is a beautiful thing. But people-pleasing is more than just kindness. Individuals who develop this core belief have a deep-seated need to not upset others. When taken to its extreme, people pleasers can become so outwardly focused they can forget themselves.

These children do not learn how to love themselves. They are taught to sacrifice who and what they are all in the name of affection, approval, and acceptance. They are trained to care more about the parent's dreams over than their own, with their parent's wishes, wants, and desires becoming an all-encompassing concern. They are brought up to believe that they are supposed to put themselves, and all they stand for, on the back burner.

These children internalize, "*this is the right thing to do,*" especially in their relationships. They often develop a misconstrued assumption that others will do the same in return and, in many cases, will accept a morsel of love, time, or appreciation as payback for their efforts. They will willingly and happily accept the dregs from the bottom of the pot.

This ongoing formative behavior imprints a pattern in the child's mind that tells them that they can only experience love when they lose themselves in the arms of a challenging person. These early life events end up controlling who they are and how they express themselves in the world, especially in their relationships. They can grow up without any first-hand experience stating what they want or need. This pattern can become so ingrained within their psyches that it can become difficult to stop. To change it for many can be downright terrifying.

You can quickly identify people-pleasers because they are your friends, your family members, your co-workers who always say, "*Yes*" when someone asks for help. They say yes because they worry about the effects of saying no. *"Will they still like me?" "Will they abandon or reject me?" "Will they get mad at me?"* These internalized questions are often amplified in an unhealed empath who, because of their ability to sense the emotions of others, will detect any unspoken projected negative energetic response.

A small shift in the energy of another can send them into a tailspin, triggering a cascade of emotions and limiting core beliefs. Their fear of conflict can be so overwhelming that they may choose to not stand up for themselves, their ideals and values, their hopes and dreams. They cave in before the game even started.

Their need to avoid disapproval, or for that matter, to prevent any unenthusiastic outcome, can cause them to say yes if only to keep energetic peace within themselves. It hurts less to agree than to say no. This need can cause people-pleasers to keep doing for others to the point of exhaustion. With some individuals, this is still not enough. The more dysfunction and one-sided a relationship becomes, with one person giving (the empath) and one person taking (the narcissist), the relationship can devolve and become plagued by codependency.

Codependency: The Ultimate People Pleaser

The concept of codependency turns the act of people-pleasing into an art form. The term codependency was initially applied to spouses of alcoholics. It identified the person who enabled the irresponsible, underachieving, or addictive behavior of another. This concept, although still valid, also includes individuals who engage in one-sided relationships, where one individual relies on the other to have their emotional and self-esteem needs taken care of.

The concept of codependency is often confused with dependency. The codependent does not rely on others to take care of their needs. They traditionally attract individuals who are dependent, unreliable, emotionally unavailable, unstable, or overly needy. They will often confuse love with pity, with the tendency to "love" people they can rescue.

Codependent individuals tend to expend all of their energy trying to meet their partner's needs and are often unable to experience happiness outside of their primary relationship. A codependent person may recognize they are sacrificing themselves, while tolerating unhealthy behaviors from their partner, but will stay in the relationship anyway. They may spend their time thinking and acting in ways to ensure the preservation of the relationship no matter the cost. Messages that might run through their minds may include:

- I am nobody without _____ in my life.
- Even though it is not perfect, this relationship is better than anything I have ever had before.
- Being in this relationship is better than nothing at all.

- If I give this relationship (or this situation) enough time, things will change for the better.
- If I change myself more, things will get better between us.

Like the people pleaser, the codependent often has low self-esteem, where they feel unlovable or inadequate. Their boundaries are weak or non-existent. Their ability to speak up for themselves and express their inner world is lacking. Codependents need other people to like them to feel good about themselves. Their deep-seated belief is that they are unlovable. This core belief will frequently cause them to enter into a relationship just because their potential partner "likes them" instead of evaluating their feelings and deciding if they like the other person in the first place.

Their negative feelings about themselves can cause them to be more willing than most to forfeit themselves in the name of another. They may also have a subconscious fear of being rejected, abandoned, or being alone. These additional factors can make it hard for the codependent to leave a toxic relationship even if they recognize how unhealthy it is for them.

Some codependents can seem needy, but others portray themselves as being self-sufficient. They will not reach out for help when they need it and frequently have trouble receiving. They will cover up their vulnerability and their need for love. Codependents are also skilled at making excuses for other's bad behaviors. They will rationalize what has transpired; blame others, and even themselves as to not deal with what they are feeling.

Codependents, more so than people-pleasers, feel responsible for solving other people's problems. Their people-pleasing coping strategy will activate as a way of managing perceived chaos. Since many times a codependent is also an empath, they have a deep desire to control the energy in their environment, thus ensuring a perceived harmony, at least within themselves.

They may help others in order to make themselves feel wanted. They may rationalize the other person cannot manage to take the appropriate action or make the right decision. They may feel rejected if the recipient does not want help or turns down their advice. Author and videographer, Lisa Romano, states that the difference between an altruistic empath and a codependent is that empaths observe and allow the other person the space to navigate their lives. Codependents feel the need to act and will often intervene in an attempt to heal the situation.

The Anatomy Of A Narcissist

The internet is full of articles about narcissism. Narcissism is a key characteristic of all Cluster B personality disorders. Cluster B personality types are selfish by nature and lack empathy to varying degrees. Their egocentric temperament is what puts individuals with Cluster B personality traits on the far right of our empathic spectrum, with individuals with full blow Narcissistic or Psychopathic Personality Disorder at the very far end of this continuum.

Narcissism, unlike empathy or empathic individuals, has been intensely studied in psychological circles because narcissists leave a morbid trail of pain and suffering in their wake.

Narcissism, in the general sense of the word, is not a bad thing. A certain amount of self-centeredness is healthy. Too little a sense of self can lead to self-esteem and self-worth issues. Narcissistic characteristics motivate us to better ourselves consistently. Without it, we would be fearful and lack confidence. It supports our ability to be driven, successful, and achieve what we desire.

So what is narcissism? The defining feature of narcissism is an excessive interest in oneself. Every narcissist has a keen sense of entitlement. The world is supposed to revolve around them and their needs. They can seem grandiose and have a profound need for attention. The people in their lives exist for the sole purpose of providing them with ongoing praise, encouragement, and admiration. What their friends and acquaintances want or think does not matter to a true narcissist. In an intimate relationship, partners of narcissists will always feel alone and neglected because the narcissists' needs will always take precedence.

People with strong narcissistic tendencies will use others to meet their self-interested needs without guilt or remorse. They choose friends based on their overall utility. They do not have the time or energy for anyone who cannot somehow benefit his or her unspoken agenda. If you do not have anything to offer the narcissist, you are no longer wanted, desired, or sought after. You will be discarded.

You can quickly spot a narcissist because of their superficially charming and outgoing nature, something they can turn on and turn off at will. You only see the caring part of their personality when they desire something from you. If their natural charisma does not work, they will blatantly lie, cheat, or steal to get what they want or to make themselves feel better. They are master manipulators who will not think twice about crossing your boundaries.

They are arrogant and have self-inflated egos. They are brilliant, powerful, and omnipotent, if only in their own minds. Since they care about themselves first, they often are bad listeners. In fact, if you are trying to discuss something important with one, you might end up feeling as if you are talking to a brick wall. They just do not get it.

They will often find ways of diverting the conversation back to themselves. They do not care to hear other people's opinions, especially if they differ from their own. They are notorious for interrupting you if you try to get a word in edgewise. They use it to control the conversation. This tactic takes the focus off them by redirecting the exchange, especially if you want to talk about an important issue or their bad behavior. This manipulation tactic makes it so they do not have to hear what you have to say, thus avoiding the dreadful thought of taking responsibility. Ultimately, your concerns are ignored.

They will maneuver you into feeling as if any problem that may arise was your fault. You will quickly find that you are the one who always ends up apologizing at the end of one of these dramatic scenes. You can argue with them until you are blue in the face. They will never apologize unless they want or can get something from you. Even if they do ask for forgiveness, that does not mean they are sorry. The bottom line, they are unable to feel remorseful for what they have done. This lack of empathy is often the most visible indicator of pathological narcissism.

Narcissists are also known to elicit fights and other adverse, hostile reactions out of people. They do this to keep getting attention. Negative attention or positive, it does not matter to these individuals. It is and always will be about them.

Narcissists, since they are better, stronger, and faster than everyone else, are envious of anyone who could potentially outshine them. They shirk mundane responsibilities. They do not and will not take responsibility for their part in any given situation. It is always someone else's fault and will quickly identify the guilty party.

When a narcissist experiences positive moments, these moments are worthy because they, and not you, are supposed to have them. Negative moments, on the other hand, are not supposed to happen and can trigger one of their most harmful behaviors, their victim mentality.

Narcissists rely on the compassion of others when things are not going their way. They will pull on your heartstrings and elicit as much sympathy from you as they can muster. They are masters of the ultimate pity party, which can suck you right into their pessimistic fear-based drama. They will contend they are being singled out, persecuted or that the world is out to get them. They are merely innocent bystanders. This mindset helps them to gain attention from those around them. People, if played right, will always feel sorry for them.

They will also vilify you if you point the finger at them. A narcissist will get angry because you are not considerate of them or their feelings. Come on! They were having a bad day. You, in turn, will become the selfish, needy, controlling, demanding, or manipulative one. They will project their feelings onto you and blame you for feeling a certain way when, in reality, those feelings were not yours in the first place.

This self-centered mentality allows the self-appointed victim to hold you responsible for all of their problems, thus diverting all responsibility from them. You are such an awful person for expecting the narcissist to live up to their word. But, do not turn the tables around. Do not expect the narcissist to come to your emotional aid if you are having a bad day.

The Covert Narcissist

Not all narcissists are outspoken and grandiose in their behaviors. Enter the "covert" or "introverted narcissist." This category of narcissists carries many of the same traits as their more extroverted counterparts, but covert narcissists are experts at concealing their true nature. On the surface, they can appear shy, humble, or anxious. They do not demand to be the center of attention but will play the victim or feel slighted if they are not. These attributes can make the covert narcissist exceedingly tricky to spot.

These individuals get their way using passive-aggressive behaviors. They will show up late, forget, or not follow through on an agreement. Instead of just coming out and letting you what they think, a covert narcissist will hint at their desires with their words and behaviors. They add self-pity to the arsenal of manipulative tools they use in an attempt to control you.

Individuals with this style of narcissism tend to be quiet and may give the impression they are good listeners. The reality is, they are just critically observing and only half-heartedly paying attention to what you are saying. They are quick to judge the value of a person or situation. If deemed unworthy of their time or attention, they will act aloof, detached, seem disinterested, dismissive, mentally tune you out, or walk away.

From the outside, a covert narcissist appears to be highly sensitive. Their feelings seem to run deep. The difference between a covert narcissist and a highly sensitive person is the fact that coverts are highly susceptible to criticism in all its forms and not much else.

All narcissists are triggered by any condemnation real or perceived, but coverts narcissists are uniquely sensitive this way. They have very thin skin. Their high emotional response can easily be misconstrued for emotional depth upon the first meeting. What a casual observer does not know is that this type of reaction only occurs when their feelings, the emotions of the covert narcissist, are involved. The tears that well up in the corner of their eyes are for them and them only.

There is one thing that makes covert narcissists stand out. It is the fact that covert narcissists are like stealth bombs. You do not see them coming. It is one thing to have someone take advantage of you when you see all of the signs and chose to ignore them. You never see it coming when talking about a covert narcissist. They will target anyone they can manipulate, especially people who are highly sensitive and insecure.

Julie Keating, in her article, *25 Signs of Covert Narcissism: A Special Kind of Mind Game*, states, "*As if it isn't bad enough that they manipulate you, make you feel bad for just about everything, and that everything is your fault, by the time you know what's going on, you're so sucked in that it becomes difficult to find your way out.*"

People who find themselves in a relationship with a covert narcissist feel confused because this subtype comes off as being kind and upstanding. Still, their actions never match their clearly stated values. People who finally extricate themselves from these relationships typically find a path of destruction where their relationship once stood. This makes the covert narcissist the worst and most insidious of the all.

Behind The Mask Of The False Self

Behind the disguise of the false self, worn by every narcissist, lies a small, vulnerable insecure, wounded child. Even though the individual may come across as being self-assured, that confidence is only a representation. It is the facade he or she wears. They live in a world where they always have to prove themselves to others and, more importantly, to themselves. Their insecurity causes them to fish for compliments, brag, and boast of their achievement or seek the applause of others. They may also appear extremely self-deprecating, where they live in a world where everyone is out to get them. These behaviors buffer the narcissist from experiencing their inner torment and lessen their deep insecurities.

They are masters of hiding who they are. The individual concealed behind the mask of the false self may initially come off as sweet, kind, or loving. Others can represent themselves as being tough, intimidating, or even scary. They can appear as caring empathic and diplomatic, but the reality is, they are not any of these things. They are just a scared child playing a role that they hope others will believe, their mask merely veiling their real cruelty.

They can only maintain their portrayal of the idealized person for so long. Some can keep up this false self for several years until they reveal their true colors, others not that long. Once their stamina for maintaining their persona falters, this is when the person behind the mask begins to appear. Their need to conceal their deficiencies, and maintain their projected self-image, causes them to employ a specific series of diversionary tactics and defense mechanisms. They will pull out their bag of tricks if you come remotely close to revealing their inner world, a world based on entitlement.

What Is Narcissistic Entitlement Really?

As you have probably figured out by now, a narcissist believes they are the end all and be all of the world. In fact, in their minds, the entire universe revolves around them, their logic and their sensibilities. Life only makes sense when viewed through the lens of themselves and their life experiences. Narcissists do not think like everyone else. Their thought patterns look something like what we find in "A Narcissist's Prayer":

"That didn't happen.
And if it did, it wasn't that bad.

> *And if it was, that's not a big deal.*
>
> *And if it is, that's not my fault.*
>
> *And if it was, I didn't mean it.*
>
> *And if I did... you deserved it."*

This brings us back to the core belief held by narcissists, that of entitlement. Narcissistic abuse recovery expert, Melanie Tonia Evans contends, *"Entitlement is emptiness, its ego – it's the dissatisfaction of never feeling "good enough" and believing "If I can just get more or control people and situations around me then I can feel better.""* Individuals who share the entitlement core belief think all of their endeavors should go as they desire, when they desire them, in the way they desire them. They believe that they should be prioritized above all others and as for you or me, no so much. We should willingly meet their needs and sacrifice ourselves all for their greater good.

All narcissists want more. It is as if they are addicted to themselves. They are preoccupied with getting what they want and avoiding what they do not want, namely dealing with their internal fear, their emotional pain, and their unfounded insecurities. They exist trapped in a place of hopelessness because their addiction is like a bottomless pit. They can never have enough, and they can never get away from their inner emotional torment and be at peace.

Regardless of what they do to feel good about themselves or regain control of their inner and outer world, the feelings never last. They are cut off from source and are unable to fill their inner coffers. They are the ultimate energetic parasite and require external resources to keep them emotionally alive. As an individual's sense of entitlement grows, like any addiction, more is needed to keep it from collapsing inward. Life in Hell for most narcissists would be a vast improvement over experiencing their true selves.

Narcissists may feel entitled to get the attention they deserve. They may feel entitled to free access to your money, your body, your online accounts, and passwords. They may subtly identify a set of rules for you, such as who you can interact with or how you should treat them.

Their importance, at least to themselves, precludes the performance of everyday responsibilities such as washing the dishes, which gives the appearance of laziness. Their energy only ever perks up when the task is something they are interested in doing. They will endlessly procrastinate anything that does not fall within their sphere of desire. They expect you to accommodate your life to suit them, jump at their requests, dropping everything to service them. In turn, your requests often go unheard. They never return the favor or express gratitude regardless of what you do for them. Getting a heartfelt apology for a wrong they commit or for inconveniencing you rarely happens either.

Their feelings of entitlement also cause them to act out, maliciously or passive-aggressively, to anything they might object to. They have no qualm in breaking the rules or crossing boundaries to get what they want. They have no regard for how their behaviors affect others and often exhibit double standards. What is good for the goose is not good for the gander. Assuming you and a narcissist are equal is folly.

Our family of origin can prepare us to live a happy and healthy life or one filled with challenges. Regardless of if your early programming turned you into an empath or narcissist; it is only through healing your inner wounds that you can ever hope to feel content in who you are.

The Dysfunctional Dance Of The Empath And Narcissist

Do fairy tales come true? As children, we are lead to believe that when we get older, we will meet the man or woman of our dreams, get married, and spend the rest of our years living happily ever after. Unfortunately, many of the long-termed relationships we enter into never pan out this way. This idyllic scenario can only occur when the dynamics between the two people in the relationship are in harmony, and working for a mutual benefit. Magic can happen in these kinds of relationships.

When an empath crosses paths with a narcissist, the relationship might start out magical, but after a short time, it can turn out to be anything but happy.

Countless people, especially ones who have found themselves in multiple toxic relationships, feel as if they have a broken relationship picker. Others may believe they are narcissist magnets. Some joke, saying that if there is a narcissist with 1000 yards, they will find them.

Wounded empaths are notorious for getting involved in unhealthy, counterproductive relationships. Many times, they cannot understand why they keep getting caught up in them, but do not look at the role they play in their formation. Narcissists do not have some strange and mysterious allure or a unique magnetic attraction that inexplicably causes empaths to become involved. Instead, they are partners in a very dysfunctional dance, one unique to these distinct personality types.

The majority of empaths can see into the heart and mind of a person. They detect the insecure wounded child that lives inside the narcissist. They might feel sorry for them because they know (believe) the narcissist cannot help being this way. They may feel compelled to help these poor helpless individuals, which leaves them feeling special and needed. *"How could the sad and pitiful narcissist survive without me?"* Their dysfunctional core beliefs propel the wounded empath forward into doing what they do best, helping their broken partner, without regard for themselves. *"They are a good person, right?"* Their need to fix their partner sets the stage for the deadly trap that follows.

The narcissist is never looking for a happily ever after in any relationship they enter. They are on the lookout for one thing and one thing only, a source of narcissistic supply. The innate sensitivity of a narcissist allows them to detect the love, light, and other unique gifts an empath brings to the table quickly. They represent a smorgasbord of tasty energy and resources upon which the narcissist can feed. Let the games begin!

The hours-long phone calls and constant texts work to draw your attention to them, and only them. This overwhelming display of attention, affection, and recognition leads the empath to believe that they have finally met their knight in shining armor, their one and only true love – their soul mate. They mistakenly interpret the narcissist's desire for narcissistic supply as love and the intensity of the connection as genuine.

The nonstop contact with the narcissist creates several problems for the empath. First, the empath becomes addicted to the affection offered. They feel happy, content, and, most importantly, loved. Additionally, the constant intrusion into their lives does not allow the empath the time or space they need to discharge the energy they have absorbed from the narcissist. Remember, empaths are emotional sponges. Their porous nature makes it harder for them to find their own space and experience their own emotions. They do not realize that they are not in the present moment but instead in the fairy tale world created by their narcissist.

The empath may find themselves perpetually thinking about their new love interest. To them, this may seem like a regular part of a budding relationship, but this is not the case. Narcissists are notorious for disrespecting boundaries, both personally and energetically. The relentless thoughts the empath is experiencing about his or her new beau are not their own. It is an all-out invasion into their personal space and auric field.

One primary reason why this mismatched union arises is because of their foundational beliefs. Both empaths and narcissists come to the romance table wounded. They both suffer from self-worth issues and low self-esteem. What brings the empath and narcissist together, into this unholy energetic match, is that they mirror each other's shadow sides, especially when talking about their core beliefs.

The term "schema chemistry" is used to describe the tendency of people to attract others who reinforce their core beliefs. Wounded empaths are driven by the subjugation/people-pleasing core belief, while entitlement is what compels the narcissists. The empath wants to give, give, give, while the narcissist is more than happy to take, take, take. As the relationship develops, they reinforce the negative aspects of each other's core beliefs with the empath becoming a bigger and better people-pleaser and the narcissist more entitled. It is a toxic match made in heaven.

This dynamic is even further enhanced if the two parties share core wounds. Through their innate sensitivities, they recognize the other and at the same time, see themselves. This acknowledgment brings hope into the narcissist's life. *"Maybe he or she can fix me."* This call for healing resonates within the empath who responds in kind. *"If I can fix you, maybe I can fix myself."*

The Dysfunctional Dance Of The Empath And Narcissist

A relationship with an empath, from a narcissist's point of view, is idyllic. Empaths are highly understanding, highly forgiving, and extremely loyal. They tend to be more accepting and less critical of a narcissist's awful behavior. If the empath is wounded, they may have boundary issues. They do not want to see their partner hurting or more likely do not want to experience their inner feelings of pain. Their people-pleasing need to care for others and their willingness to settle for crumbs is perfect for an individual who will begrudgingly oblige.

Life could not be better for a narcissist than hooking a really wounded and highly sensitive empath. They have finally trapped someone who will willingly take on the mental and emotional burdens the narcissist does not want to own.

The dance between a narcissist and an empath can go on for years. As long as the narcissist has a handy supply, they will continue the dance. Dancing is easier than therapy and does not require the narcissist to heal. As the empath works to solve their partner's problems, the narcissist will find more problems the empath can fix. This vicious cycle can continue indefinitely.

Wounded empaths are naturally more vulnerable to this type of parasitic personality. If an empath chooses to remain in a relationship with a narcissist, they must take responsibility for their part of the dance. As they say, it takes two to tango. What are they bringing to the table, and why? The glaring truth of the matter is not that the empath is attracting narcissists to them, but that they are keeping them longer than someone who is emotionally secure. Ouch.

The Lifecycle Of A Narcissistic Relationship

The consistent and abusive conduct displayed by narcissists comes complete with its own vocabulary. Words often associated with these individuals include false self, love bombing, future faking, gaslighting, projection, cognitive dissonance, devaluation, smear campaigns, flying monkeys, and hoovering. These behaviors can appear in any of their relationships but are even more apparent in a narcissist's most intimate ones.

If you believe you might be in a relationship with a narcissist, flashing lights and sirens might start to go off in your head as you read about all of the odd and peculiar deeds you may have experienced.

There are three predictable relationship stages most narcissists move through idealization, devaluation, and finally discard. Each stage has its own sets of tools and tactics the narcissist will employ. There are the tools they will use to get you hooked, ones will they use to control and manipulate you, and ones they will engage in as they get ready to move on from the relationship.

Love bombing and future faking are used early on in a relationship. The narcissist can reintroduce them when they experience relationship discord. Gaslighting, projection, cognitive dissonance, and devaluation are utilized to protect the person under the mask or to increase their feelings of superiority. Smear campaigns, flying monkeys are tactics that are availed upon to save face or as a means of controlling those around you. Finally, a narcissist will hoover once the relationship has ended, where they will use it similar to love bombing to suck you back in.

The Narcissistic Relationship - Part 1

The goal of a narcissist is to get you hooked so that you will enter into a romantic relationship with them. They leadoff their courtship endeavors with love bombing and future faking. These techniques appear during the beginning or idealization stage of relationships. If you are not sure when this is, this is when you first meet, and they open their mouths.

Love Bombing

Communication between the partners in any relationship is normal and healthy. It takes time to get to know one another, and there is no better way to do this than by spending time together, either in person or by phone. Email, social media, and texting have made our ability to keep in touch even easier by providing additional and often instantaneous platforms where contact can take place.

When a narcissist meets a new, potential love interest, the first tool in their bag of tricks is something referred to as "love bombing." Love bombing is a form of mind control. The narcissist will bombard you with excessive communications, be they frequent and extended phone calls, endless texting, emails, or a strong desire to meet often in person, all in an effort to monopolize your time.

Their behavior can be easily confused as someone who is extremely interested in you. You might envision your new friend as a hopeless romantic or believe that you have finally met Mr. Right. These early interactions may seem wonderful, sexy, and exciting. You might enjoy the ego-stroking flirtation they provide and be left believing that a unique and special bond is quickly forming. The specialness you are feeling can be potentially dangerous if you have self-worth issues.

Love bombing is done to keep your attention focused on them. It tends to move a relationship forward very quickly while beginning the process of disconnecting you from your friends, family, or other support systems.

The intensity of fake love they project can cross into your auric field and past your boundaries. They are masters of invading your space, which makes it hard to separate your thoughts and feelings from theirs. This ploy makes it especially challenging for empaths who more readily detects and receives subtle energy information from others.

Future Faking

Once the dialog has commenced, narcissists pull out yet another tool from their extensive arsenal, "future faking." Future faking is how the love-bombing narcissist sucks you in. They trick you into believing that you are meant to be together, that you are soulmates. They will begin to layout your future together from this happily ever after position. It is all rainbows and unicorns as you learn about the beautiful life you and the narcissist will have.

They will take all of the information you volunteered during the love-bombing state and turn it around on you. They will speak directly to your heart's desire. They will provide you everything you have wanted all along. Unfortunately, it is all a big lie. All narcissists are pathological liars, and they are very good at it. They will lie right to your face in such an authentic way that you end up believing them.

They will also use future faking to keep you in the relationship once things sour. They do this to keep your hopes alive. They will promise a myriad of things that ultimately will never happen. They will deceive you with the fantasy that one day, the dreams they promised will finally come true.

Task number one is complete. The narcissist has succeeded. Through their beguiling skills, they have trapped you. They have successfully knocked you out of your body and you are off somewhere in the ethers dreaming of your potential future with them.

The Narcissistic Relationship - Part 2

Life with a narcissist often starts wonderfully. They will use your happiness to maneuver you into a position where you are bound to them, making it more difficult to leave. They might convince you to quit your job, live together, get married, or have children. In any case, whatever ruse they use, you are now in some way dependent on them and under their control.

A fundamental shift, from who you thought they were, to their true self, emerges when the relationship is secure in their mind. It is common for the spouse of a narcissist to claim that everything was going magnificently, that is until they said, and "I do". Then everything changed, and all bets were off.

You might have gotten sick, were busy at work, or had a child. Regardless of the cause, you were no longer able to afford your significant other the same kind of attention you once were. This is when the narcissist's insatiable need for admiration begins to surface. They will go from being kind, supportive, understanding, empathic, and loving to something else. This grace period can last for a few months to several years. The day will eventually come where the mask begins to slip off, and you get to see the person behind it.

Once they feel their importance decreasing, or their control diminishing, all of the bliss you were initially experiencing will change. All you might do is criticize them, challenge them, or stand up for yourself. Narcissists do not take any of these perceived slights well. Anything that puts their personality, their performance, or their fragile egos into question can set them off. They are prone to defensive, angry outbursts, especially if they do not get their way. They will overreact to situations and make you regret you ever said anything in the first place.

Whatever you might say or do, from the most straightforward comment to confronting them about one of their numerous lies, can set them reeling in an all-out effort to protect their perceived view of themselves. Then you will be honored with the opportunity to experience the narcissist in their purest form. You have now entered into the devaluation stage where they will withdraw their kindness and instead punish you; many times will full-fledged attacks. They will unleash a barrage of abusive and manipulative tactics include gaslighting, projection, cognitive dissonance, the silent treatment, and even physical abuse to regain control.

Gaslighting

"Gaslighting" is a form of emotional manipulation where the narcissist questions your memory of an event or causes you to question your own. They may pretend to forget promises or deny something that happened, including situations or conversations. They may secretly hide or rearrange your belongings, adding to your mental confusion. All of these things can cause you to second-guess yourself, your memory, and your sanity.

The real sign of gaslighting appears in the numerous confrontations you have with a narcissist. They may put down your friends and family members, causing you to doubt your relationship with them. Their goal is to get you to withdraw from them to gain increased control over you. They may reframe what you say to make you sound like the bad guy. They might bring up a sensitive topic, accuse you of something or make a mean or off-colored statement about you just to get you riled up. Suddenly, you find yourself in an argument you did not intend to have.

Any discussion will quickly devolve into a crazy-making, chaotic, mind spinning drama, which is all designed to wear you down and punish you. Many times, these cruel and disproportionate attacks, referred to as "narcissist rage" are designed to destabilize, discredit, frustrate and confuse you. The manipulation techniques they employ can set your mind on fire, trying to figure out what is going on, or what you did in the first place.

You will find yourself saying the same things repeatedly, apologizing profusely, yet regardless of what you say or do, it has no effect on dampening the situation. When you finally think you have talked things out, they will turn around and begin discussing the issue once again, ignoring any previous conversations.

Sometimes they will restore a glimpse of the false, kind, and loving person you initially fell in love with, all in an attempt to control you again. If that does not succeed, they will turn around and begin insulting the parts of you they once idealized. You are left wondering who you are talking to and what their true feelings are. You may question, "*Does he or she actually feel this way?*"

These crazy-making conversations will leave you feeling drained as if someone has sucked the life right out of you. This tactic will also leave you off guard and off-balance, which makes you easier prey. If you take their bait, they will have managed to uncenter you and interrupt your body's ability to ground. Instead of being strong and sure, your internal defenses are now weak and vulnerable. This tactic grants the narcissist even more power over you and your energetic environment.

You might find yourself ruminating over what just happened for hours or even days. You might commit to yourself to enter into these discussions diplomatically but quickly discover that you are feverishly defending yourself and your honor. Their mastery of confusion is impressive.

Projection

We have already discussed the unconscious defense mechanism of projection earlier. Narcissists turn projection into an art form. Their submerged feelings will rush to the surface when you challenge the false self, or they are experiencing a painful internal moment. This primitive defense mechanism will go into full gear and right into deflection mode, which ensures two things. They will punish you for challenging them, and you now become the person who has committed all of these atrocious acts. Whatever he or she is feeling is put onto you and are identified as your thoughts, feelings, actions, and behaviors.

The unhealed parts of the narcissist are screaming out for attention. They project their feelings instead of looking inside and owning them. They cannot take responsibility for them. It is easier to dump their faults and failings onto you rather than look in the mirror.

Cognitive Dissonance

We experience cognitive dissonance when someone says one thing and does the opposite. Wikipedia defines as follows: *"In the field of psychology, cognitive dissonance is the mental discomfort experienced by a person who simultaneously holds two or more contradictory beliefs, ideas, or values. It is triggered by a situation in which a person's belief clashes with new evidence perceived by that person."*

In a narcissistic relationship, it often experienced as the stress, anxiety, or uneasiness felt when trying to hold two or more contradictory beliefs. The relationship starts with the love bombing and false futures but then changes and you begin to see their other self, their true self. If you are not up on the complex behaviors of the narcissist, you are left confused, questioning if the person you cared about had any feelings for you at all. It is hard for anyone to wrap their minds around the notion that what you just experienced, what you once believed about your partner, was all just a huge lie and a masterfully played out con-job.

You have lived in a lie of their creation and are left wondering, are they Dr. Jekyll or Mr. Hyde? Are they abusive, or are they reasonable? Their newly revealed selves conflict with your established sense of reality about them. You end up not knowing who or what to believe.

If you are unaware of this kind of behavior, you might opt to ignore it, while internally praying that they will change or that things will be better with them down the road. Sometimes it is easier to dismiss what is going on and hope the problem will go away. They love me - right?

Accepting the truth of who your narcissist is and what is actually going on is tough. If you exhibit the core belief of subjugation/people-pleasing, you might find yourself in a trap that is hard to escape. You may find yourself doing anything to please the abuser instead of angering him or her. You might reason it will create less emotional pain to excuse their offensive conduct rather than getting angry over it.

Researchers suggest that the awful feelings associated with cognitive dissonance are why many abuse victims stay in a relationship with an abuser.

The Silent Treatment

When all of the narcissist's tricks of the trade are exhausted, or if they are too lazy or tired to deal with someone or a situation, they will employ the "silent treatment." The silent treatment, as the name implies, is when the narcissist will no longer take your calls or reply to your texts. If you are in a living arraignment with them, they will give you the cold shoulder or act as if you do not exist. They will not engage, leaving you feeling like you were dropped like a hot potato. The silent treatment may go on for days, weeks, or longer. They will disappear physically or emotionally without providing a reason why.

A narcissist will use the silent treatment as a form of punishment for going against them or their ideals. They may use it as a way to avoid discussing pressing issues, gain the upper hand in the relationship, or as a means of getting increased control. They might describe their abusive behavior as "giving you space" and utilize it to avoid supporting you physically or emotionally. Sadly, many times, they will employ it to free up their time and energy to be with someone else or to pursue a new potential supply.

The Narcissistic Relationship - Part 3

Once you see behind the mask, Part 3 of the relationship commences. It is called the devaluation stage. With it, discard is inevitable. In essence, they begin formulating their escape strategy before ultimately dumping you. It might take months or years for this to occur. You walk around on eggshells during this phase of the relationship, never knowing what kind of sadistic fun and games are waiting for you around the corner. If you tolerate the narcissist's bad behavior or look the other way as they seek out a fresh supply, you might not get discarded right away, but it will happen.

You are misguided if you believe that accepting the horrid conditions they put you though it will save your relationship. They will not see your actions as an indicator of your love and commitment to them. Putting up with their ongoing abuse only causes them to have even less respect for you and can cause their cruel behavior to escalate. You have taught them well. You have shown them that you will not withdraw your love and affection regardless of what they say or do.

Remember, the whole relationship has nothing to do with you. Narcissists look for partners who will idealize them and do things solely for them without question, resistance, or commentary. They are not interested in building a life with you, as they may have suggested during the initial phases of the relationship. That was all just a lie to get you hooked.

In between their vicious attacks, you might receive some love bombing, with the associated future faking in a manipulative attempt to regain control and trick you into not ending the relationship prematurely. They do this because they are either not quite ready to get rid of you or because they have not lined up and secured their new narcissistic supply.

Words often associated with the discard phase include smear campaigns, flying monkeys, and hoovering. These are used to manipulate those around you, your coworkers, your friends, and families. Narcissists use these tactics to make themselves appear like the helpless victim of you, the evil, manipulative, controlling bad person.

Smear Campaigns

A smear campaign is an intentional effort to destroy you and your reputation, where they will tell the people closest to you, or for that matter, anyone who will listen, how awful you are. They will use it to point out all of the mean and nasty things you did to poor pitiful them. A smear campaign is enacted to protect their false self and reduce exposure of the man behind the mask. Their consummate lying skills have been known to trick some people into believing their all-out deceit.

Flying Monkeys

Flying monkeys are often individuals who have been manipulated by the narcissist to inflict additional torment on you. Typically, they are kind, empathic people who believe the charming lies the narcissist spreads during the smear campaign stage. These individuals think they are helping the hapless victim. In reality, they are being used to spy on you or to spread gossip. Many times they have no idea they are being manipulated as part of the narcissist's overall plan of destruction.

Hoovering

Once the relationship has ended, the narcissist will attempt one last ploy to suck you back in. This technique is called "hoovering." Hoovering characteristically occurs after the silent treatment or during a period of no-contact. They will call you, text you, send an email, or show up at your home or office with the desire to communicate with you. If you reestablish communication, they will lie, lie, lie. They will profess their undying love for you, promise you it will all be different, or how they now recognize their part in why the relationship failed. The door once open to them will only return you to another cycle of chaotic abuse.

If you fall for their hoovering tactics and get sucked back into the relationship because you fell for the false future they promised, remember - if you keep having the same issues with the same outcomes followed by the same promises, the relationship will never change. This sad but true outcome is because deep down, the narcissist has no desire to change who or what they are.

The Thrill Is Gone
Now That You've Lost That Loving Feeling

Ending a relationship with a narcissist is anything but easy. It can be as mentally and emotionally exhausting as dealing with them on a day-to-day basis. You would think by saying, "*it's over*" they would get the message and move on. Not so with these people. Narcissists hate losing their supply, especially on short notice. They do not go gently into the night, especially if they are not done with you.

Now granted, there are times when a narcissist will choose to leave. You may have decided it was time to take care of yourself and began refraining from playing their mind-numbing games. Your newfound resolve can quickly cut off their supply and their desire to be with you. You might have gotten sick or incapacitated, which would mean they would have to take care of you versus the other way around. Perhaps your job, your family, or the myriad of responsibilities your narcissist dumped on you, leaves you with little time or energy for them. Any of these things can cause a narcissist to exit stage left. How the relationship ends, like the patterns of behavior they exhibited in the formation and devaluation stages, also follows a clear cut pattern.

By in large, the vast majority of dealings with narcissists come to an end because they have crossed a line in which there is no return. You might have caught them cheating on you. You might be tired of their perpetual lies, their crazy outbursts, or their incessant need for attention and adoration. Regardless of what they did, their entitled and erratic behaviors broke the proverbial camel's back. You are done, finished, finito.

You may want to head out the door, but there may be practical reasons why you choose to stay. You may not be able to support yourself or your children financially. You might be sick. Your inner wounding, your fear of being alone, of not being loved, or of never finding Mr. Right might activate. A narcissist is an expert at triggering you, your limiting core beliefs and dysfunctional attachment style. They might keep you trapped through a mixture of hope and fear.

Then there is everything else that comes with trying to conclude a relationship with a narcissist. There is the pitifulness that exudes from their pores and fills the air. The overwhelming emotions they project, combined with their ongoing fanciful promises to change, can overpower your senses and sensibilities, especially if you are an empath. This overwhelming bounty of lies and boundary-crossing emotional energy can cause you to change your mind.

Research suggests it can take up to seven tries to walk away from an abusive relationship. You are not alone if you are having a difficult time ending it once and for all. It takes a great deal of strength and inner courage to break free.

If, for whatever reason, you decide to reengage your narcissist, you might initially think things are getting better. The world is looking brighter. Your narcissist is, at long last, acting like a healthy, caring, and compassionate human being. You might think they finally get it and are starting to live up to their promises and potential.

This revived golden period, sadly, will not last for long. You can be pretty confident it is only a matter of time before all of their well-masked inner demons will be back. The fake future they presented will come crashing down around you, leaving you back at square one. You might experience disbelief and cognitive dissonance as you reenter the crazy-making devaluation stage again.

Hopefully, it will only be a matter of time before you realize enough is enough. Throughout the nightmare of your life with your narcissist, you knew something had to change. Now you understand that regardless of what you do to fix things, they will never accommodate you or the changes you desire. This internal mental shift can put you into the position of perceiving your relationship from a different perspective.

You may begin to gain insights into what is truly going on instead of living in the fantasy world of how you hope things will be. You may start to acknowledge all the sacrifices you have made and hoops you have jumped through, all in the name of love. You may begin to recognize all of the time and energy you have invested in them and the relationship. You may come to realize that after all you have put up with, you still do not have the relationship you wanted, the one they promised to you.

The thought of a life happily ever after may begin to fade from your mind. You may start to see beneath the dream and recognize it for what it is - a bill of goods. You may begin to question if your narcissist ever loved you in the first place. You may start to evaluate their hurtful words and their erratic behaviors and conclude, *"If this is love, then I don't want it."*

There are only two ways of moving forward from this place. You can accept them for who they are. This resolution requires you to acknowledge the fact that you will be spending the rest of your life walking around on eggshells and navigating the minefield of their nightmarish behaviors. The compassion required to survive in this sort of relationship, without completely losing your sense of self, rivals Mother Teresa.

The other choice is to cut your losses and run.

The Addiction Of Trauma Bonds

Typically, when a couple decides to go their separate ways, there is often a feeling of finality. You have the opportunity to say goodbye, grieve, process what has happened, pull yourself togethership, and move on. Not so with a narcissist. Breaking up with one can be gut-wrenching. It can leave you, and your world, feeling turned upside-down. It can require you to conjure up every bit of inner determination you can muster to go and stay gone.

You may assume when things get really bad that you will have enough strength to leave. This ability to walk away and stay away can be especially challenging for individuals who grew up in abusive homes. They are often conditioned to believe that abuse is only physical or perhaps sexual. Anything else is just a normal part of everyday life. They are often unaware that the head-splitting and mind-numbing time they spent with their narcissist was unadulterated abuse. Long-termed abuse of this kind can cause a form of Stockholm syndrome to develop. When tied to a relationship, it is commonly referred to as "trauma bonds."

Trauma bonds form through repeated cycles of abuse with intermittent cycles of positive reinforcement. The body produces high levels of cortisol, an adrenal stress hormone, during periods of turmoil. Increased levels of dopamine, the feel-good hormone, are released when a reward, such as kindness, is offered.

In essence, we become addicted to the emotional and hormonal highs and lows we experience at the hand of our abuser. A bit of benevolence after a long afternoon of dealing with your partner's narcissist rage can trigger an intense dopamine release. The dramatic emotional peaks that follow a traumatic episode are what make the good times seem so remarkable. This hormonal high can keep you trapped and coming back for more.

This pattern of intense pain followed by amplified perceived pleasure deregulates our internal hormonal state making it difficult to make logical decisions and manage our emotions. This addiction can create a profound need to see them once more, hear from them once more. *"My world would be better if only he or she would text me."*

You will miss them while you are out of their sphere of influence. You might romanticize the relationship or worry about what you might be missing. You might find yourself struggling to figure out what just happened to you or trying to understand what you could have done better.

You might also find yourself obsessing over many things instead of being in the present moment. *"What are they doing now?"* *"Am I going to hear from them?"* *"Does he or she still care about me?"* Your inner wounding will be running on overdrive. The level of toxic rumination you will experience, as you try to make sense of the conflicting memories you have, can be all-consuming.

Then, like every other time, you have tried to walk away, you see them or hear from them again, and they turn on their charm and begin making promises they will never keep. You get to bask in their attention and affection one more time with the hope that the person you initially fell in love with will return. You breathe a sigh of relief. You fall for the prospect that maybe, just maybe, the relationship will work out, and just like that, you can become hooked again. The manipulative games they play can be intoxicating.

Some survivors of narcissistic abuse suggest that it is easier to go through heroin withdrawal than it is to end a relationship with a narcissist. Breaking a trauma bond is not easy, but there is a road to recovery.

Narcissistic Withdrawal

The narcissist, like you, will also begin to experience withdrawal symptoms once you cut off their supply. The shortfall of your life force energy can cause them to do one of two things. Initially, they will come back if there is even the slightest chance of getting a fix from you. They will reappear

The Thrill Is Gone

with guns blazing with their old, charming, or perhaps pitiful, needy self front and center. They will start another cycle of love bombing and offering grandiose potential futures.

They may seem deeply wounded by the break-up, displaying what may appear to be genuine emotions. They will tell you how much they love you and try to convince you that you have made a colossal mistake. They will remind you of all of the extraordinary times you had together, or all of the astonishing thinks they have done for you. They might develop a newfound illness or devise some problems only you can resolve. They will "want to talk" or will find some other pretext to communicate.

Do not be fooled by their desire to reignite the romance. It is not an indicator of their unbridled love for you or their desire to be with you. These acts are only a thin veneer that covers over the fear they are experiencing from the potential threat of losing their supply. Any response you give them will feed their addiction.

They will resort to one of their tried and true devaluation strategies if their charm, coaxing, and persuasion do not work. They will try to guilt or intimidate you. They may become cruel, abusive, or lash out and do bizarre things. You will get to experience their rage once more. From an outsider's perspective, it seems counterintuitive for the narcissist to employ spite filled tactics in their quest to get your undying love and attention again, but they do.

The Dysfunctional Dance Of The Empath And Narcissist

If this strategy also does not work, they will immediately start looking for their next source of supply that is if they have not already been working on that front as well. A narcissist will walk away and never look back once they secure a new victim. You might think to yourself, through your anger and your pain, that it is finally over, but if their new supply rejects them, they may reemerge.

Most narcissists do not need time to heal after a break up and will latch onto another empathic, compassionate, loving, patient, supportive person fast. Do not let this upset you. Do not assume that your relationship was so bad that it was easy for them to forget about you, move on, and find someone new. They do not hurt. They do not mourn. They are parasites. They will go out in search of a new supply once the one they have been feeding off of is exhausted. It is their nature. It is what they do.

Let us talk for a moment about your now ex-narcissist's new partner. Their new beau will be drawn to them for the same reasons you were; their charm covered pack of lies. The fresh supply in his or her life does not know the truth; they do not know what is real and what is an illusion. They do not see the person behind the mask, yet. They are basking in the addictive attention and affection the narcissist bestows in the early part of their life-cycle. Blaming him or her does you no good, so do not be jealous. Yet there is nothing more devastating than seeing your ex smiling brightly on social media with their latest recruit within weeks of your separation.

Exit Strategy

Not everyone is in the position of leaving their narcissist right away. If you have the means to go, do so. Get out of Dodge! For individuals who have children still in the home, ones who are not in a financial position to do so, or who are involved with a volatile physically abusive narcissist, you may need to form an exit strategy. Having a physical and emotional safety plan in place can help ensure you have a secure place to land once you walk out the door.

Get your finances together. If you are not working, find a job. Open a separate savings account and start putting money away you can use to carry out your escape. If you feel unsafe in opening an account in your name, perhaps you can get a friend or family member you trust to open one for you.

If you are in a particularly abusive relationship, and have no means of independent support, investigate a domestic violence shelter. If you think the potential fall-out will be horrific, you might consider moving to another city or even state. This extra step may be required if you believe they will come looking for you and punish you for leaving. Whatever you do, do so quietly. There is nothing worse than a narcissist who may have to face one of their worst nightmares, the threat of losing their supply

There is also something essential you need to know if you invited your narcissist to live with you in your home. Depending on state law, even if they do nothing or pay nothing in support of the house or household, you may need to go through eviction proceedings to get them to leave.

Your home is considered "their home" even if only your name is on the lease, deed, or mortgage. They are not considered a guest if their physical mail comes to your address. You may have to serve them with a notice of eviction legally, and this can take up to 30 days to finalize. Unless there are signs of abuse or other specific qualifying factors, the courts will not grant a restraining order, and you are left dealing with a narcissist who is aware of your intentions. Not a good situation by any means.

No Contact

One widely recommended rule as you try to break free from a narcissist is the concept of going "No Contact." As the name implies, going No Contact means precisely that: no contact **whatsoever**.

That means you should not meet with them in public or private locations. Block their number on your phone to stop any unwanted calls or texts. Add their email address to your black list so that any incoming messages go directly into your spam folder. Delete them on social media. Also, beware of any potential flying monkeys who could be used to reach you if you have friends in common. You might have to apply the No Contact rule to these individuals as well.

Going No Contact may seem harsh, but it is vital. You are vulnerable during the early stages of your recovery. You are hurting inside. You are in the beginning phase of ending your addition to the cycles of abuse and reinforcement, which will cause you to want one more fix, one more high, from your abuser. You may still be susceptible to their manipulation tactics.

Imagine, out of the blue, a text from them appears on your phone's screen. You vow to yourself that you will not look at it, but for some reason, you cannot help yourself and cave in. Your now former lover sent you a cute picture or is checking in to say hi. Regardless of what transpires in these communications, you have just self-medicated. If you have gone through this process before with another narcissist, you might recall the calmness you experienced after one of these messages. It feels amazing. But it also pulls on your heartstrings and can potentially cause you to rescind on your decision to end it.

Sometimes our addiction is so intense we can rationalize breaking No Contact. You might want to get in the last word and let them know what you really think. You might want to let your former lover know how much they have hurt you. You might want to tell them to get a life and leave you alone. Regardless of the cause, they got what they wanted. You responded. You just gave them another fix.

On a separate note, if, for some reason, you left something at the narcissist's house, let it go. Forfeiting your favorite sweaters, or some DVD's, is a small price to pay for your sanity. They will hold your possessions hostage coming up with one excuse after another why you cannot pick them up. This only works to string you along and keep the lines of communication open.

Do not expect them to come running to collect any possessions left at your house, either. They will "try" or "work on" getting them till the cows come home, which may not be for another 20 years. Taking decisive steps to eliminate and eradicate their belongings from your living environment may be needed.

Bless your heart if you have children together. Dealing with child custody and visitation could mean years of unavoidable contact. Thankfully, there are a few things you can do to minimize your exposure. First, reduce ways in which they can communicate with you to one medium. Insist on emailing instead of texting. Another concept that you can use in situations like these is a technique called "Gray Rock."

Going Gray Rock is often employed when you are unable to go No Contact. You can also use it if you are still cohabitating with your narcissist and have not been able to implement an exit strategy.

When you Gray Rock, you keep any and all conversations to a minimum. If they ask a question, try to respond with simple yes or no answers. If a longer reply is necessary, keep it short and sweet. Never engage in small talk. Never tell them how you are doing. And, never, ever, ever ask them a question. Any of these things can open the door to further dialogue. You would be surprised at how quickly an exchange can escalate from pleasantries and go to places you are emotionally unprepared for. If they want to chit-chat, do not take the bait.

Rising From The Ashes

It is over, done. You have said your last goodbye, moved out or got your toxic lover to leave your home. You have blocked them on your phone, on social media and can no longer receive their emails. You have done all you can do, but now you find yourself sitting home alone in a whirlwind of tangled thoughts and uncertain emotions. "*What am I going to do now?*"

The absence of your partner can create a gaping hole in your life. It can feel like a massive void within the depths of your being, a vacuum of nothingness that was at one time filled with his or her energy. The longer you were together and more your lives were intertwined with one another, this sensation can be even more intense. You not only lost your significant other, you have also lost someone to share your life with, traumatic as it may have been.

You may not be prepared for the intensity of emotions you are experiencing or how fast your mood changes. It may feel like a rollercoaster ride, but like any good rollercoaster, the dramatic ups, and downs, in the beginning, will become less intense as time goes by. You may find yourself having a hard time thinking straight, eating, or sleeping. These feelings are a normal reaction to loss, change, and transformation. You are entering into a period of withdrawal. Your neurotransmitters, including dopamine, endogenous opioids, corticotropin-releasing factor, and oxytocin, are dysregulated and in a state of flux. If you are not running at your best right now, give yourself a break and cut yourself some slack.

You may also be experiencing a sense of relief at having escaped an abusive situation, but that understanding does not lessen the emptiness you may feel inside. You may think that life, as you know it, is over. You may feel robbed of your time and energy or that you have wasted years of your life. You may feel as if life has gotten you again, where it has set you up for another cruel round of intense suffering. You may find yourself mentally vacillating between "*I love this person*" to "*They abused me. I cannot go back.*" You may wonder, "*Will I find someone else?* Or "*Will I end up all alone for the rest of my life?*"

Everything is disrupted during this time, your routines, your responsibilities, and even your identity. It is a period of uncertainty where your future, which may have been apparent in the past, is not as clear cut as it had been. It is essential to remind yourself as you move into this stage, "this too shall pass." The ending of a relationship is not a life sentence for the rest of your existence. It is a temporary state filled with ups, downs, and everything in between.

It is during this highly sensitive period that you might be tempted to get back together with your narcissist friend, regardless of how destructive the relationship was. Sometimes, a terrible situation is easier to manage than dealing with the unknown and the potentially overwhelming emotions and brain chemistry changes going on inside you right now.

You might be inclined to resort to one of your old coping strategies. You may choose to suppress your feelings by pushing them down or moving them as far away as possible. You might instinctively try to escape your anguish by creating distractions and excuses to numb your inner turmoil. You might decide to bury yourself with work, drugs, or drinking. Whatever your diversion of choice is, avoiding and ignoring your pain will not make it go away. It will not change your propensity for making unhealthy relationship choices. Avoiding only opens the door to making the same mistakes again.

The agony you are experiencing, on the other hand, can be used as a catalyst for change. The dynamics of this challenging time offers you the opportunity to emerge on the other side of it as a different person as a "Wounded Healer."

The term Wounded Healer refers to a person who has undergone intense pain and suffering and used these injuries to transform him or herself. They emerge from this profound transformation more in touch with their authentic inner nature with a greater awareness of themselves. These individuals become a source of wisdom and inspiration for others.

Swiss psychiatrist Carl Jung coined the term Wounded Healer. Jung was interested in how myths and symbolism seemingly permeate our thinking on conscious and unconscious levels. He suggested that within our collective unconscious, there exist a series of archetypes, patterns of thoughts and images that are universally present in the human psyche and can be recognized by all. One of these archetypes is the Wounded Healer.

Jung links the Wounded Healer archetype to Greek mythology and the story of Chiron. The myth tells us that the nymph Philyra, to avoid being raped by the god Cronus, transformed herself into a horse. Cronus, discovering her deception, likewise changed himself into horse form and had relations with her. The result of this union was Chiron.

Chiron was a centaur. Centaurs possess the upper body of a man and the lower body of a horse. He, due to his divine parentage, was immortal and could not die. Shamed by his appearance, Philyra abandoned him. Sources suggest the god Apollo, the god of inner illumination and healing, adopted him and taught him the healing arts. Chiron, later in life, was accidentally struck by a poisoned arrow from Heracles' bow. Chiron does not die from this injury. Instead, he suffered excruciating pain for the rest of his life. It was because of his inner and outer wounds that Chiron became known as a legendary healer in ancient Greece.

Like Philyra's abandonment of Chiron, the ending of a relationship, especially a toxic one with a narcissist, opens the door to the emergence of the Wounded Healer and the beginning of an inner journey of change. It can feel as if we are dying when we enter into this cycle of healing. It is the dark night of the soul. It is when we hit rock bottom or reach a crisis point in our lives that real, lasting change occurs.

In it, we willingly chose to go into the depths of our own inner hell, where we are forced to face and re-experience our old wounds. We get to acknowledge the part we played and the choices we made in our life's dance. This new awareness allows us to learn from our mistakes and avoid repeating them in the future. It is through this process that the old self dies and a new self emerges. A more expansive and empowered self is born. We will never be the same once we begin this journey.

This process offers us the opportunity to feel the feelings (the original wound) that were too distressful to deal with the past. We may have been too young or too afraid. The dynamic of the Wounded Healer allows us to finally comprehend what has happened to us and release the limiting belief systems we created as coping mechanisms. This newfound perspective will enable us to create a new expanded paradigm to live by. We emerge from this experience stronger, wiser, and knowing ourselves better.

It takes a considerable amount of courage and inner strength to delve into the depths of the soul and be willing to explore our repressed trauma and pain. We have to be willing to face the terror of who we truly are and be open to not knowing where this inner exploration will take us. It forces us to let go and stop trying to manage its outcome.

Individuals who journey down this road are recognizable by the scars they bear. These scars are not scars of defeat, but scars of victory. Each attests to a battle won and a victory achieved. They proudly let the world know, "I survived."

Are you ready to follow the path of the Wounded Healer?

The Journey To Me-dom

The ending of a relationship with a narcissist remarkably does offer a number of positive attributes. You no longer have to cater to their wants and needs. You no longer have to spend countless hours ruminating about what they did or worrying about what they might do. You no longer have to battle with the raging beast or walk around on eggshells. It is astonishing how many hours there are in a day when you do not focus your entire world on the black hole of a human being you once viewed as a friend or lover. It frees up a wealth of mental and emotional time.

With all of this reclaimed energy at your disposal, you can shift your focus from them to YOU. You can work to fill the void you may be experiencing with enjoyable activities or use it to broaden your horizons by exploring new interests. Refocusing your world and your priorities will help lift you out of your funk and fill the empty space you are feeling inside.

Shocking as this may be, it is your job to make yourself happy. You do not have to earn happiness. It is something that you are innately entitled to. You will never find it in the arms of another person, contrary to what you may have been led to believe. And if you have discovered you are a bit of a people pleaser, here is another morsel of insight. It is all right to put your needs first.

You might be thinking to yourself, *"but, but, but, if I put my needs first, wouldn't that make me a narcissist?"* There is a vast difference between loving and caring for yourself and narcissism. It can be summed up with one word: motivation. To start, you are an empath. This innate proclivity is not something you can lose. No one can take this away from you. Selfishness and greed do not align with your inner world and clash with your integrity.

Narcissists ensure their needs are met first, period. Empaths, especially healed empaths, can discern when to take care of themselves and when they need to step up to the plate and act selflessly. Your ability to feel the emotions of others will always let you know when those around you need it most. Taking care of yourself is not a selfish act. It is about considering your needs, your wants, and your desires. It is about giving yourself the time, energy, and level of consideration you would willingly give others.

The path to healing is not a simple one. It is a journey into the depths of your psyche and your soul. It is about change and transformation. It can liberate you from the limiting core beliefs that may have controlled you your entire life. These same beliefs may underlie why you got involved with a toxic person in the first place. The caring and compassionate qualities you project out into the world act as a beacon calling every self-centered individual to you from miles around. It is no wonder why so many wounded empaths find themselves in one unhealthy relationship after another.

It is one thing if you found yourself sucked in by an exceptionally gifted covert narcissist. It happened once, and you learned from the experience, kudos to you. If, on the other hand, you have a predisposition for getting involved with insalubrious people or discover a pattern of participating in dysfunctional relationships, then perhaps it is time to make some changes to your inner world and break yourself free from the cycle of abuse.

If you are unsure if you are inclined to attract narcissists into your life, take a moment to reflect on not only your current relationship but all of your close associations, past and present. This evaluation should include your intimate relationships, your close friends, and your family of origin. Starting with your current affair, allow yourself to move back in time to review the dynamics of those closest to you using the list below as a general guideline. Examine each of them from your newfound understanding. Perhaps it is time to start to make some changes in your life if a pattern emerges.

- What was the relationship like?
- Were you able to be you while with them?
- Did you forfeit yourself, in the name of love or friendship, for this person?

- Did you find yourself accepting things that deep down bothered you?
- Did you feel manipulated so he or she could get their needs met?
- Were your needs met?
- Did you feel loved, accepted, nurtured, and cherished?
- Do you see any similarities to other relationships you have had?

Is a pattern developing as you evaluate your past relationships?

Starting Over

You do not have to live a life filled with pain and sorrow. It is not your life calling to fix every broken person on the planet or tolerate chronic bad behavior. The repetitive cycle you may be finding yourself in does portray one thing. It is letting you know that a part of your soul is wounded and in need of healing. You have already started the process of becoming a whole magnificent person. You did this by owning your early life history, by identifying your core beliefs, and your defense mechanisms. As we move forward, you will have the opportunity to rework yourself from being broken into being filled with the bright light of your authentic self — a true Wounded Healer.

You might think you are too old to change, that who you are is set in stone. You may buy into the adage that you can't teach an old dog new tricks. Scientists have proven that we can make profound changes in our lives regardless of our age. Called "neural plasticity," research shows that our brain is continually being shaped and molded by all we encounter.

Everything we experience, including our thoughts and emotions, are converted into electrical signals that activate different parts of our brains. These signals travel through channels known as "neural pathways." A neural pathway is a connection between nerve cells in different parts of the brain. The more certain nerve cells communicate with each other, the stronger the pathway becomes. Every time we think the same thought or react to a situation in the same way, we deepen our established neural pathways. The workings of neural pathways form the basis of our habits and appear in our lives as repeated patterns of thoughts, feelings, and actions.

The development of neural pathways is most active in children. If you grew up in a healthy household, with a secure attachment style, robust neural pathways might have formed that support feelings of happiness, joy, safety, and optimism. If, on the other hand, you grew up feeling unworthy, unloved, unappreciated, or insecure, the newly developing neural pathways can become stuck in negative belief patterns.

Our neural pathways are like well-traveled hiking paths. The more you go down one path, the better defined and more worn it will become. It becomes the most familiar and most straightforward road to travel. Emotionally, these well-worn paths become our kneejerk reaction to life events. It is the place our brains and bodies instinctively go. It is the path of least resistance and operates effectively behind the scenes on unconscious levels. This mechanism explains why we may feel bad and not understand why. It is because our brain and body are operating on autopilot.

Fortunately, we can change our thoughts and begin the process of creating new neural pathways. Imagine, instead of automatically experiencing fear, anxiety, dread, or overwhelm to life events, your kneejerk reaction is to feel happiness, contentment, or bliss. It is true! We can transform our beliefs and beliefs systems and move them from a life of scarcity to one of abundance and success.

This process of change can happen, but not without effort on your part. It takes time and energy to form new neural pathways, but this work will help liberate you from chronic negative thought patterns into healthy, happy ones. You will be challenged to confront your existing beliefs about yourself and your old habits of responding to life events. Opening yourself up to this level of healing will provide you with a choice: You can pick a new road to follow, or you can keep going down the same tried and true path. I hope you chose wisely.

As we move forward, we will be addressing a multitude of different areas, each of which will support you in your endeavors. So with each step, you take, be open to the new you emerging on the other side.

The journey to wholeness requires that you look honestly, openly, and with courage into yourself, into the dynamics that lie behind what you feel, what you perceive, what you value and how you act. It is a journey through your defenses and beyond so that you can experience consciously the nature of your personality, face what it has produced in your life, and choose to change that.

- Gary Zukav

Addressing The Fear Of Change

Fear is the emotion that traditionally keeps individuals stuck in negative patterns. It inhibits our ability to grow, change, and become the person we want and know we can be. When we fear speaking up for ourselves, being alone, or doubt our ability to care for ourselves, it can act as a death grip keeping us trapped in untenable situations. It forces us to tolerate life events that should cause us to walk away. It can trick us into putting part of ourselves on hold, so we do not have to experience the symphony other emotions that may be triggered.

We all experience fear at one time or another. Fear can keep us from hurting ourselves, but it can also have a limiting effect on our behavior. Your mind, especially if you grew up in a dysfunctional family, may be filled with subconscious thoughts of recurrent traumatic experiences and the associated negative repercussions tied to them. You may also experience it as you look to venture into uncharted ground, especially when the outcome is unknown.

It was once said, "*Fear is the thief of dreams.*" The reality of this sentiment is enormous. Fear takes away our choices. It can keep us from doing the things we want or need to do for ourselves. It constrains us and can end up ruling our lives. It consumes our energy leaving us experiencing unexplainable stress or frustration. It can also cause us to feel stuck with no place to go.

Our fears can manifest as procrastination, where we choose to do nothing. Sometimes we go into resistance, where we dig our heels in and grasp tightly onto our current position. We may go into denial about our fears, choosing to blame others or the situation for our choices. We may also decide to avoid putting ourselves into scary situations, thus eliminating any possibility of a threat.

Addressing our fears is all about choices - you can choose to move forward, or you can choose to stand still marking time. Many of the time, our fears have nothing to do with any real threat or danger. The only peril we may face come from our own thoughts and ideas, ones we conger up in our minds.

Fear is like a scary old-time black and white movie poster of the Werewolf or Dracula hanging on the back of a door in a darkened room. You want to leave the room, but the only thing you can see, as you try to navigate your route, is this scary creature obstructing your passage. What you might not realize at that moment is that the threat is not real. It is only when you turn on the lights that you can see that it is only a picture and poses no danger at all.

As you sit in this darkened room, unable or unwilling to step through the door, you will never know what is on the other side. Your reservations, worries, and uncertainties will keep you trapped forever. You will never appreciate the freedom and sense of power that you gain as you move through its limitation and into the light of a new day.

Addressing our fears is a significant component in overcoming them. By illuminating the darkened room, the unknowns become known, what was once scary becomes mundane, the overwhelming, trivial.

Miraculous things happen to those who consciously choose to overcome their fears. You may discover long forgotten feelings of inner strength and self-confidence. You may gain certainty in your newfound skills, abilities, and even your downfalls. You may have the good fortune of learning more about yourself, your wants, needs, and desires. These insights can open the door to a world filled with opportunity, enjoyment and happiness.

It can feel uncomfortable and downright scary when we make profound changes in our lives. In the context of healing our inner wounding, we have to risk putting ourselves out there for people to see instead of hiding who we are. Growing up, you learned to sequester your genuine reactions and your innate spontaneity. You became afraid to expose your true self to have some semblance of security. Who you are on the inside may have all but disappeared, leaving only a shell of who you once were and can potentially be. The only thing stopping you is your fear, and as you now know, most of the things we fear are illusions.

Will The Real Me Please Stand Up?

When we are congruent with ourselves, our inner world matches our outer world. We are our "authentic self." Being our authentic self is about reconnecting with who we are. It is about being true to ourselves. It is about having our thoughts (inner world), words, and actions (outer world) match. It is about honoring our feelings and having the confidence to express them, despite external pressures. We feel at home inside our bodies when we are authentic. Researchers suggest that our ability to be authentic to ourselves and others is linked to our happiness.

It is easy to be a people-pleaser when you have a hard time being authentic. Individuals who are controlled by their fears and their inner wounding find it challenging as well. It can be terrifying to do or say things that go against the norm, the tried and true, and in the case of relationships, what you think your partner wants. "*Will he or she still love and accept me if I speak my truth?*" "*What will happen if I say no?*" Then there is the guilt, the need to avoid conflict, and valuing others over ourselves. Massive amounts of fear can bubble up right before you share your inner world, especially if you have little to no practice in doing so.

Being authentic allows us to love and accept ourselves at our core, to do what makes us happy, and to follow our passions regardless of who we may disappoint. Doing so leaves us vulnerable, but at the same time, allows for the creation of genuine, intimate relationships filled with unconditional love.

You have to be willing to take an enormous risk in showing your true self, complete with all of your imperfections, shortcoming, and insecurities. You have to embrace who you are instead of who you think you should be. You also have to be prepared to love yourself enough to accept the costs and consequences your words and actions may elicit from others, which may include ending a relationship that is unhealthy for you.

If you think about it, you have spent the better part of your life operating based on a series of false beliefs. These beliefs made you feel as if you were somehow inadequate. You learned to say and do things to keep the peace and make others happy. If you want to experience happiness in your life and create a healthy relationship with someone special, you have to be willing to let go of the false beliefs, which are not serving you. Use this period of change and transformation to risk letting go of old emotional patterns that have kept you trapped in damaging situations.

The Four Selves

Our sense of self begins to develop as soon as we exit the womb, if not before. Our life experiences shape and mold how we see ourselves. Each of our successes and failures contribute to our life story. But who are we? Many of us do not know. We can only see ourselves based on our perceived role in society. We apply a label to identify ourselves based on our job function. I am an engineer, teacher, scientist, housewife, or mother. These descriptions do not offer any genuine, substantive information reflective of our unique internal character, which brings us into the realm of "self-esteem."

Self Esteem

How we perceive and value ourselves is the textbook definition of self-esteem. Our place in society defines part of it, but it also includes our appraisal of ourselves. We trust ourselves and our abilities, skills, talents, and wisdom when we have healthy self-esteem. We can see all of the things that are uniquely ours. This view is honest and realistic. It allows us to accept responsibility for our actions and even our mistakes. It enables us to respect ourselves, love ourselves, and forgive ourselves without judgment.

People with healthy self-esteem take pride in their accomplishments and are unaffected by what is happening outside of themselves. They display wholeness of their psyche and are congruent with themselves. Traits of someone with healthy self-esteem include:

- The ability to like and value yourself as a person.
- The ability to show kindness and compassion towards yourself.
- The ability to recognize your strengths.
- The ability to make decisions and assert yourself.
- The ability to move past your mistakes without blaming yourself unjustly.
- The ability to try new or difficult things.
- The ability to take time for yourself.
- The belief that you matter and are good enough.
- The notion that you deserve happiness.

If your self-esteem is low, you may continuously tell yourself that you are fat, lazy, stupid, selfish, inconsiderate, or unworthy. The number of negative things we may perceive about ourselves is limitless. Our "inner critic" is responsible for these kinds of intrusive thoughts. We can say some of the most awful demeaning things to ourselves, things we would never say out loud to anyone else. Instead of looking at the gifts we bring into this world, we focus our attention on our perceived flaws. Our inner critic is an expert at finding our weaknesses. Then we work feverishly to gather evidence to support our dysfunctional internal beliefs.

We all have different skills and abilities. We might be good with numbers. We might be an excellent dancer or cook. We might have great organizational skills or can band people together around a common goal. We cannot be and do everything. No one can. We automatically assume that others, if they excel in one area, must excel in every area of their lives. Regardless of how well you know someone, you will never fully understand how they feel or perceive themselves.

Actor Robert Downey Jr. is known for his many iconic film roles, including his portrayal of the comic book character Iron Man, the mastermind British detective Sherlock Holmes and the silent film star Charlie Chaplin. Downey, early in his career, despite his critical acclaim and widespread notoriety, fought with substance abuse issues.

But by 2001, after a series of arrests and unsuccessful drug treatment attempts, he said: "*You know what? I don't think I can continue doing this. And I reached out for help, and I ran with it.*" He had to deal with the devil and face his worst critic, himself. What inner demons he had to conquer to regain his sobriety, we will never know, but his success in healing his internal wounds is a lesson we can all take note of.

We can become trapped in a cycle of low self-esteem when we underestimate ourselves or ignore all of our positive characteristics and traits. Low self-esteem can make it difficult for us to understand why anyone would like us. We may find it hard to receive a compliment because, on the inside, we do not believe the kind things others are saying to us. The words spoken are incongruent with our reality.

You can challenge your inner critic. You can use it to see yourself for who you are rather than judging yourself on who you think you should be. Who established these internalized goals in the first place? Who told you that you were fat, stupid, lazy, or unlovable?

What Does Your Inner Critic Say To You?

Self Worth

Intrinsically tied to self-esteem is the concept of "self-worth." Self-worth is defined as *"the sense of one's own value or worth as a person"* or as *"a feeling that you are a good person who deserves to be treated with respect."* When you are not able to be you, if you cannot be your authentic self, your self-worth is always effected.

The concept of self-worth is often used synonymously with self-esteem, but they are not the same. Self-worth is not about our view of ourselves, but more concerned with appreciating our intrinsic value and our inherent worth as a person. It is the recognition that we are good enough regardless of if we are smart, talented, successful, or funny. We believe we are loveable and can make a positive impact in the world. It is the sense that "I matter" at minimum to myself.

Our self-worth is like a diamond that resides in the center of our chests. This precious diamond can become covered over with our judgments about ourselves after years of internalizing our negative thoughts. We add another layer of film and filth to our diamond each time we find new evidence to support our internal beliefs. After a while, we can no longer see the bright, beautiful person we are on the inside. All we can see is the distorted image we have created.

Your diamond may appear lacking in luster instead of shining brightly within your being. It may look crusted over or covered with barnacles. It may seem impenetrable as if a brick wall or a solid piece of dark corroded stainless steel surrounds it. If you try to interface with it, it might tell you to go away and leave it alone. It might say to you that you are hideous or a monster. It might inform you that you are unlovable, unworthy, or a failure. Whatever you may see, feel, or experience when you chose to interface with this aspect of yourself, recognize that the hurtful insights you believe you are receiving from it are, in reality, a reflection of your lack of self-worth.

The diamond of your self-worth, believe it or not, always shines brightly. It is the essence of who you are and holds the highest quality of your being. It embodies the distinctive traits you incarnated onto the Earth bearing. You can never diminish the innate quality and intrinsic characteristics of who and what you are. It can get covered over and hidden from view, but its light is still shining beneath the muck and mire. It is the core of our being and never goes away.

Self What? Self Love

We are not born with an owner's manual. We are not taught how to love and honor ourselves or differentiate between what is beneficial for our overall wellbeing from what is toxic. We were tossed out onto the sea of life left up to our own devices and charged with figuring out how to navigate its troubled waters. If someone only explained to us how to have a fulfilling existence instead of becoming experts at creating a life filled with pain, suffering, and sorrow, our stories would be different.

If you could step outside of your body and watch how you treat yourself, what would you see? Are you good to yourself? Kind? Loving? Or do you beat yourself up, deprive yourself of things you want or deserve, self-sabotage, create unrealistic expectations, abuse your body, or make destructive choices? Each of these things indicates a lack of love we have for ourselves.

What does loving ourselves feel like? It is about treating ourselves with kindness, concern, and compassion. It is about not judging ourselves harshly or punishing ourselves for every mistake we make. It is about being warm and understanding, recognizing our inadequacies and imperfections, and responding to them with the same level of support and respect we freely offer others. It is about liking who we are, lock, stock, and barrel.

If you find that you do not like yourself, much less love yourself, that is ok. You have spent years battling an inner bully. It is the well-worn pathway your mind reactively travels down. Do not beat yourself up now. You have just put your toes down onto a fresh patch of grass and began creating a new way of being, a new way of seeing and a new way of reacting to life and its challenges. The journey to loving yourself calls for dedication, devotion, and practice. It takes time to build a love muscle, one that can securely embrace you every minute of every day.

We naturally love ourselves when we have appropriate self-worth and self-esteem. These things allow us to be internally whole and let us interact with the world as our authentic selves. There is one other thing that we require to love ourselves. It necessitates we move beyond our fears. It involves getting out of our heads and into our hearts. It calls for us to engage with that tattered, worn out, barnacle-encrusted, beat up diamond we have on the inside. It demands us to have the courage to feel our feelings and honor them, regardless of where they may lead.

Self love will compel you to act with your best interest in mind and challenges you to ask, "*Why not?*" As they say, whatever does not kill you will make you stronger. Imagine the inner strength you will develop as you flex this muscle. It is easier to accomplish long-lasting and permanent changes when we engage ourselves with love rather than trying to motivate ourselves through shame and blame.

Buddha once said: "*You can search throughout the entire universe for someone who is more deserving of your love and affection than you are yourself, and that person is not to be found anywhere. You yourself, as much as anybody in the entire universe deserve your love and affection.*"

If you have not loved yourself up until this point, you might find this comment a bit hard to hear, but over time, you will recognize its truth and wisdom.

Self-Care

We live in a whirlwind of activity with a multitude of tasks to complete daily. We can become so caught up in the hustle and bustle of our lives that we can forget to love ourselves. Loving ourselves feeds the soul, renews our inner resources, and recharges our batteries. It refuels us, rather than being one more thing that takes from us. Through it, we can experience peace, wholeness, and balance in our lives.

You can think about the benefits of loving yourself in another way. Imagine your time, energy, and inner resources as money in the bank. Every time you do something, such as take care of one of your hundreds of responsibilities (or your narcissist partner), you are withdrawing money out of your account. Now granted, smaller tasks like washing dishes, doing laundry, or filling your car with gas may only cost a few cents. Our lives, however, are filled with highly involved complex situations and circumstances where we can almost feel our inner reserves running dry.

When we give to ourselves, instead of drawing money from our coffers, we are depositing into them. We repay ourselves each time we do something loving. Even 15 – 20 minutes a day of me-time can bring about incredible changes. You can watch yourself blossom if you resolve to love yourself.

Once more, you are probably saying to yourself, "*Nooooooo, I do not want to be a narcissist*." And again, loving yourself and taking care of your happiness is not a selfish act.

It is a loving act. You are loving yourself. If you have spent much time with a narcissist, you know from experience that they are not going to love and nurture you or aid in your happiness.

The things you can do for yourself are endless. It does not have to be big or earth-shattering. You can take a hot bath, get your hair cut, or relax with a massage. Take yourself out on a date. Go shopping or to a movie, eat at your favorite restaurant, or go away for the weekend. Any of these activities can help to recharge your batteries.

Then there are things you can do that are not activity-filled but still support your inner resources. Meditate, read a book, close your eyes and breathe deeply or journal (a topic we will be delving into in more detail shortly). You can even take a nap or stay at home and do nothing if you want to. The important thing is to ask your inner self what it wants and what it needs. Then, be open to receiving and following its guidance.

You might also want to surround yourself with people who feel right to you and support your happiness. It is all right to let go of or take a break from individuals who only withdraw energy from your inner reserves. Just because you were friends ten years ago does not mean you are required to maintain contact. You are growing, and you are evolving. Your internal shift may cause some of your relationships to fall by the wayside. If you find this happening, pat yourself on the back. It is a leading indicator reflective of the changes you are making.

There is no need to worry or feel sad about what is going on. Letting go of the old opens the door for bringing the right people into your life, people who are more in alignment with who you are now. It is appropriate to grieve the loss. In the end, relish in all you will be gaining in the weeks and months to come.

Doing loving things for yourself, in the beginning, maybe something you will have to plan actively. It does not just happen. It too is a choice, so chose you! Mark your self-care plans on your calendar. Creating a self-care schedule will help increase your commitment and keep you on track if you are having difficulty finding the time.

There is one notion that does need mentioning when talking about loving and caring for ourselves. You might decide to go to the gym, do tai chi or practice yoga to help recharge yourself. Whatever you choose to do, if after a while you do not like it or it becomes a burden, quit doing it. Listen to your inner directive. You will not obtain the healing benefits the activity initially offered if guilt or a sense of obligation keeps you committed to it. Forcing yourself to do something can transform what was once healing into another task, another job to complete. Instead of paying into your bank account, it ends up withdrawing from it.

Finding Your Bliss

How do you uncover what floats your boat, brings joy into your life, helps support your self-care activities, and affords you bliss? Bliss comes in all shapes and sizes. It is not about having a new car, a fancy house, or the latest gadget on the market. It is about feeling content in the things you do and the life you lead.

We experience bliss when we are engaged in something we love doing. When we are passionate about our endeavors, we feel great inside. We will happily spend hours upon hours working on it, refining it, not because we have to, but because we want to. It can bring joy, fun, enthusiasm, and a sense of purpose to your life. The challenge in finding your bliss is discovering what makes you tick. What brings you joy may be completely different from what provides others a sense of satisfaction.

Many people grow up not knowing what they are passionate about. Finding your bliss is about exploring yourself, your likes, and dislikes. There are so many things you can try. The only thing standing between you and your happiness is your willingness to give it a chance. You may uncover something you relish on your first try, or it may be your hundredth. It is about the journey. Take the time to investigate a variety of diverse ideas until you find something you love.

You do not have to quit your job to find bliss. You can experience pleasure in the simplest things you do, the silliest things you try, or the most out-there things you endeavor.

Once it starts to emerge, it cannot help but filter through into the regular and more mundane aspects of your life.

It does not matter what it is you do. From gardening to skydiving, the sky is the limit. The important part is that you are doing it for you. Taking the time to nurture yourself is one of the healthiest things you can do to live a happy life. Then, when you have your batteries charged, you will be able to care for others in a balanced way. The time you invest in yourself is always time well spent.

You are still stuck and uncertain of what to do? Here are some ideas that might stir your imagination. Your bliss might be in the making as you explore one of these things.

Take a class

Sometimes when we are unsure of what we want to do, taking a class might help to get your creative juices flowing. Whether at your local community college or one that you find online, try it! You might discover that you have a knack for cake decorating, water painting, computer programming, dancing, or writing.

Attend a Meet-up group

Meetup groups have popped up across the country. You can find them in large urban areas and smaller communities. Many are free or have a low cost to attend. There are Meetup groups that focus on self-improvement, spirituality, and health and healing. There are Meetup groups for the politically minded, for exploring religious ideas and ones for individuals who are just looking for some stimulating conversation. There are even Meetup groups for singles!

Trek the great outdoors

Go camping. Take a walk in a park. Climb to the top of a mountain. Learn to identify the birds you see, the plants you encounter. Lie out on the grass and watch the clouds go by. Enjoy the solace of a star filled night. You might find yourself invigorated and lusting for life after spending some time in the great outdoors.

Explore your kitchen

Have you ever baked a loaf of bread, made cookies from scratch, or tried a recipe that sounds tasty and inviting? Our kitchens can hold many unseen wonders, lost to prepackaged convenience foods. Handcrafted meals always cost less to prepare than their mass-produced counterparts do. They are healthier for you and invariably taste better. You might discover that cooking up a four-course meal for a group of friends or your family is fun and perks up your appetite for life.

Plant an herb or vegetable garden

Planting a garden, be it herbs or your favorite vegetables, can be rewarding and satisfying. As your plants grow and mature, it will be a constant reminder of the mysteries and wonders of the world. You might say, "*But I do not have a back yard to plant them in.*" Anyone can start a garden in a brightly lit window or in pots on a patio. Imagine how amazing it would be to eat a homegrown, organic tomato or season your meal with a bit of basil or cilantro you grew. An increasing number of community gardens are also popping up, where you can rent a plot of land and grow your favorite delectable delights.

Start a spiritual practice

Have you always wanted to begin meditating, learn tai chi or yoga? Maybe you will find bliss there. If you live in a rural community, there are hundreds if not thousands of books and DVDs available online, which can help get you started. Also, an overwhelming amount of free information online can answer your questions, provide you with some insights or point you in the right direction. *Why do you hesitate, Grasshopper?*

Volunteer your time

You might discover that you will find bliss in assisting others. Countless organizations are on the lookout for good dependable people to lend a hand. The limitless number of people that you will be serving, even if you only volunteered a few hours a week, could be staggering. Help build a house, cook in a soup kitchen, or lend an ear on a support line. Each of these can be rewarding.

Sometimes we find bliss in some of the weirdest places in areas that we did not know existed or would never have imagined trying. Pay attention to strange synchronicities that pop up in your life. You can also receive insights into satisfying your needs and desires when you tap into your intuition and the message of your soul. They can guide you to the perfect thing for you and your happiness.

The Messages Of The Soul

Your intuition is always there ready to help you, be it in finding your bliss, or uncovering the direction your life should take. It can ignite the fire of your passion. You may find yourself willing to take on tasks you may have thought unattainable in the past. Anything is possible if you listen to the guidance your intuition provides.

We have all had situations in which we were trying to resolve a problem. Then out of nowhere, seemingly clear out of the blue, we know the solution. This is our intuition at work. Our intuition acts on one basic principle. If you ask a question, you always get an answer. It works 100% of the time. Your query can be from any area of your life you are seeking understanding.

These insights come in several forms. They can come to you as a thought that seems to magically appear out of thin air, yet feels very solid and defined. You might see a series of images flash in your mind's eye. Your inner voice might suggest you do or try something. You might be provided with the knowledge you are seeking while watching something on TV, as you read a book or in a dream. You may find yourself talking to a stranger, and the conversation seemingly provides you with the answers you need.

Many people feel inspired, motivated, and will often want to start on their new endeavor right away after receiving this kind of guidance. Try not to ignore it, edit it, invalidate it, or otherwise pooh-pooh what it is or where it may be coming from. Instead, accept it, relish it, and thank the universe for its reply. While you may not have all the answers at that moment, the direction or task it presents will always feel right – that is, until our ego gets involved and tries to sabotage it with our negative thought patterns.

One thing about paying attention to your intuition is the fact that spirit nags. If you find yourself asking a question multiple times and receive the same answer, this is a clear indicator that spirit is trying to communicate with you. It is endeavoring to get your attention. Granted, we should not act on everything we may feel inspired to do. Sometimes our mind will try to play tricks on us, but once you have an idea, you can quickly check its veracity.

With a potential direction in hand, bring it down into your heart center at the fourth chakra. Check-in with yourself to see how it feels. Does it feel good to you, or is there a part of you having a problem with it. When we do not feel congruent with the answer we received, perhaps the concept is not right for us. Maybe we are experiencing fear in some aspect of our being.

To help find the underlying cause of your resistance, try asking yourself a series of questions such as:

- What benefit is this to me?
- Is there any part of me that is having trouble with this?
- Is this the right direction for me to be heading?
- Is this achievable, and if not, why?
- Is there anything getting in my way that I need to address before I move forward with this?

If other questions come up for you as you work through this process, ask those as well.

The Dr. Rita Rule

Another effective way of determining if what you are thinking or feeling inspired about is right is "The Dr. Rita Rule". The Dr. Rita Rule states, a "*Yes*," is Yes, and a "*No*," is No. If you ask yourself a question and internally hesitate, receive a "*maybe*" or an "*I don't know*," then the answer is in actuality NO. The confusion creeps in when we try to rationalize a No response in an attempt to change it to Yes. So if it feels blasé or there is some aspect of it that does not feel right you, honor the No.

Inspiration Blockers

Several things may interfere with your ability to connect to your soul and act upon your intuition. You might envision the objective as being unreal or unattainable. Rather than considering the idea, you might write it off right from the start. If your concept seems convincing, you may try to talk yourself out of it. You may allow your inner doubts, judgments, and lack of belief in yourself, turn what was once gold into led.

Sometimes the subject of our inspiration seems perfect. Internally, we decide to follow our inner directive. We begin to think, plan, and massage the idea around in our heads. Inevitably, a time comes when we have to implement it. As we look to realign our energies to support the work ahead, we may find that we are unable to break free from the responsibilities of life, real or imagined. We may tell ourselves we do not have the time, energy, or resources to continue. Our inherent lack will always shut down the forward movement of an idea.

At other times, we might be all fired up to incorporate this great new and exciting thing into our lives, and regardless of our best intentions for some reason, our get up and go, gets up and leaves us high and dry. We are unable to exert the energy required to manifest our dreams.

Our fears are what traditionally stand in-between us and our ability to bring our dreams into reality. We may fear what we desire is unattainable. We may worry that we are not capable enough. We may fear that we will lose control, or we will fail. With so much potential fear interfering with our ability to achieve our goals, you may ask, "*Why should I bother paying attention to spirit at all?*"

Where would we be if we were not open to following our intuition and the directives of the soul? Cave dwellers would never have chipped away at rocks to make our first tools. There would be no pyramids, and there would be an empty field where Stonehenge stands today. We would still think the world is flat, and the thought of walking on the moon a fantasy. We would not be able to look upon the smile of the Mona Lisa or be enthralled when we hear Tchaikovsky's 1812 Overture. Progress, whether through art or industry, would come to a grinding halt that is if it ever got started at all!

Inspiration is what drives us forward. It transforms dreams into reality. It provides us with hope and is a vehicle for transcending ourselves and our current condition. Best of all, it is something that comes built into each of us.

By listening to and following the guidance your intuition provides, you are opening yourself up to phenomena you may not have known existed or may have seemed impossible for you to access in the past. Let your inspiration take you to new heights, propel you forward into new adventures, or ignite your passion for creating a bigger and better light bulb. In whatever direction you find yourself going, enjoy!

Mindfulness

Many of us live our lives on autopilot. We exist day to day programmed like an automaton and never considered the choices we have. We let our old habits dominate what we do and what we think. We have walked down the same familiar, well-worn path for so long that we assume this is what life is all about. We unwittingly accept it and do not believe it can be any better or different. We can become so entrenched in our old habits that we do not even realize that we are not living but are only surviving.

You may start to detect patterns of negative thoughts invading your inner world as you begin to focus your time and attention on yourself. Our runaway disparaging thinking can unequivocally influence our ability to moderate our pain and suffering. When we indulge in unhealthy notions, we reinforce our negative feelings about ourselves, which chips away at our self-esteem. These thoughts are not new. They did not come about because you ended your relationship with your narcissistic partner. They evolved over time and throughout your life. It is only now that you are turning off your autopilot that you may be noticing them.

We often assume hundreds, if not thousands, of thoughts fill our minds all at the same time. The fact is we can only have one singular concept occupying our brain at any given moment. The constant barrage of ideas, opinions, and beliefs passing through our awareness are all competing for the same mental slot available in our consciousness.

Said simply, if you are thinking about your upcoming adventurous outing with friends, then that is your one thought. In turn, if you are obsessing about how your ex was a downright dirty scoundrel, then this is the thought filling your solitary cognitive spot. We can get confused because our thoughts can jump from one concept to another at lightning speed, but only one idea can take front and center within our awareness at a time.

This small detail of how our mind works can be exploited to support our healing. We can employ it by purposefully redirecting our one thought from a destructive intrusive one to anything of our choosing. We can achieve this by paying attention to our inner environment, our thoughts, feelings, and body sensations and making a conscious choice about what to do with them at any given moment. The act of raising our awareness and paying attention to what is going on inside is called "mindfulness."

Mindfulness

Mindfulness, by default, puts us into the present moment. It causes us to draw our attention back to what is going on in the here and now. This simple change can transform you from the inside out.

We are responsible for what goes on in our inner world, just as we are responsible for our happiness. You may not know what it feels like to be happy and whole inside your own skin at this time in your life. You may find yourself in a chronic state of fear, "doing" instead of "being." When we are being, we are not running around taking care of chores, or trying to solve the mysteries of the universe. We are one with ourselves, wholly, and at the same time, relaxed. When we are being, we just are. We are right here, right now, not in the past and not in the future.

Being is not procrastination. Weird as this may sound, being IS doing. You are being. You are allowing things to move and transform into a new state, a state where the ego is released, and you no longer have to use your energy to propel you forward or hold you back. A mental notion, a belief, or an expectation does not form the basis of your life. When you are being, you are going with the flow of the universe and not pushing your agenda forward, whatever it may be.

This state of existence may feel uncomfortable. You may be accustomed to knowing what your next step will be or having your life planned out months in advance. It is reasonable not to know. When we are being, we have taken a step back from the working of the brain. We have opened ourselves up to the guidance that our soul provides. When we are being, we recognize that we are not in charge, and we cannot control the outcome of any given situation. We are allowing, allowing the energy of the universe to travel through us uninhibited. This free flow of energy permits our lives to unravel on its own terms.

From this place of objectivity, we can see that resistance is not the way to go, but at the same time, we may find that investing more time and energy (unless prompted) into our affairs is not right either. We discover that the best way of dealing with any situation is to let go of any presupposed notion of how it should be and allow it to unfold before us. Any decisions we may have to make, in turn, will seem harmonious to us, regardless of how hard they may appear.

Sometimes when we are in this place, we are led to do things that can, to the rational mind, seem like a complete mystery. We may find that we are guided to faraway places or are compelled to open the door to possibilities we may never have imagined before. At other times we might unknowingly put ourselves into situations that on the surface may seem traumatic, painful, or at odds with ourselves, but as time passes, we will often look back at these moments and recognize their perfection. Regardless of what it is, we work to accept what life hands us with open arms.

If you are not sure what it feels like to be one with yourself, try this exercise:

- *Take a nice deep breath.*
- *That is right; breathe in through your nose to the count of five and slowly out of your mouth.*

- *Again, in through your nose and gradually out of your mouth.*
- *As you continue breathing, notice how your body feels.*
- *Where are your thoughts focused?*
- *Calmly, observe them without judgment.*
- *Simply keep breathing.*
- *On your next breath, as you slowly exhale, relax your body even more.*
- *Permit yourself to effortlessly let go of all the tasks you believe you should be doing right now.*
- *Acknowledge any negative thoughts that might rise to the surface.*
- *Say hello to them and release them as well.*
- *Allow your higher self to illuminate all the could have's, would have's, and should have's you are carrying around in your body and your auric field.*
- *Let them go also.*
- *Now, on a slow exhale, release any emotional charge or guilt attached to them.*
- *It is unimportant to know precisely what the specific items are. Know that your psyche can and will help you achieve a perfect place of relaxation within your body. It will support you as you find your ideal state of beingness.*
- *Give yourself a few moments to fully discharge all that you have been holding on to.*
- *When you are ready, notice how your body feels now. Is it more relaxed, calmer, or more peaceful?*
- *What about your thoughts? Have they settled down?*

- *Take one more deep breath and have these good feeling, the wonderful feeling of peace and calmness radiate throughout your body, mind, and soul.*
- *Acknowledge how good this feels.*
- *Take one last breath and ask that this state of being stays with you throughout your day.*

This state of peace is what "being" instead of doing or reacting feels like. There is a sense of inner calmness that words cannot adequately describe. People who feel emotionally safe tend to do better when trying to find this place within themselves. They are not battling with intrusive thoughts or raging emotions. Mindfulness can be used to help you feel this way regularly. Wouldn't that be wonderful!

Mindfulness Practice

If the peace and serenity of beingness is the goal, where are you now? We all have moments when life events disturb our inner world. Depending on what it is, we may be able to quickly recover our composure and return to our normal healthy, and happy state. At other times, situations can set something off within us which we may find challenging, if not impossible, to shake off. If you think about it, when you are caught up in a cycle of worry or rumination, you are bogged down, living with an inner world filled with pain, shame, self-criticism, or judgment. You are not happy. You are hurting.

When you are feeling anxious, upset, hurt, or frustrated, there is a disruption in the force. One of your inner wounds, a previous trauma, or a negative core belief may have become activated. There may be a conflict between what your authentic self wants and the precepts stored in your unconscious mind. You still may be trying to fit into the square box society, or your early programming, has erected. It may also be an indicator that you are in an abusive or toxic situation, especially if you consistently find yourself being negatively affected at the hand or mouth of another.

Any of these things can cause a disturbance within you. You may find yourself, when this occurs, reactively responding to the situation using a primitive defense mechanism or caught up in a cycle of negative thought. We can, notwithstanding, use these moments to become our own private detective and solve the mystery of what is happening.

Identifying what set you off can be challenging to determine. You can, nevertheless, ready the stage for profound healing by getting to know what elicits your negative responses. These insights might help you learn how to react to scenarios that once distressed you with more mature coping mechanisms.

When you begin a practice of mindfulness, you will quickly discover that you are not your thoughts. You are not your fears and not your insecurities. You will start to notice that it is just energy, an emotion, stimulated in you. We never respond to something emotionally unless there is a conscious or unconscious thought tied to it. From this position, you can begin to observe your thoughts and embark on connecting the dots between them and your emotional responses. It is okay to be with your thoughts and experience your emotional state. You can do it without reacting to them or judging them. It is easier than it may initially sound.

We reinforce our unwanted or intrusive thoughts, the more we think about them. They can become trapped in our one empty mental slot and arouse similar negative thoughts and emotions. It can be like the ball in a pinball machine. Our negative thinking can begin bouncing off the bumpers of our other false beliefs and inner wounds until our insides are shouting *"TILT! TILT!"*

You can start the process of calming down what has flared up and hopefully let go of the rest by being mindful of your thoughts, especially your intrusive ones. They can be easier to control and even prevented if you catch them early on instead of waiting until you are in the midst of a full-blown meltdown.

Mindful Meditation

One way of supporting our ability to "be" is through meditation. Some people suggest that self-improvement techniques such as meditation or mindfulness are hard or even exhausting. What is even more taxing on your body and your soul is the underlying stress negative thoughts and emotions can have.

Many meditation practices use mindfulness as their foundation. When we think of meditation in the west, we envision an Indian mystic dressed in a colorful robe sitting in a lotus position on the top of a mountain. We may long to experience the blissful states reported by these holy men but may find it personally challenging to achieve. This perception of meditation causes many to shy away from even trying it or giving up not much after they have begun.

The goal of meditation, like mindfulness, is to focus our thoughts on a single solitary item. When we immerse ourselves in one task or one thought pattern, we end up losing track of everything else around us. Controlling what the mind focuses on allows any intrusive thoughts that may be vying for our attention to slip gently away. This practice helps to calm the first chakra and supports our body as it discharges harmful energy and emotions.

What many of us do not realize is that two different types of mindful meditation can be employed. The first type of meditation is called passive meditation. This relaxation technique is what we often envision when we try to meditate. Passive meditation incorporates methodologies such as repeating a mantra or affirmation, focusing on our breath, or clearing the mind of thought. It is not the breath, the mantra, or even the act of keeping the mind clear that supports healing. When we focus our minds on something, anything, it fills our empty slot. It has the added benefit of helping us detach from the sometimes uncontrollable dynamics going on inside.

Many passive meditation techniques can leave us feeling as if we are unable to meditate at all or that the skill is beyond us. We close our eyes, and within minutes, if not seconds, our mind starts to wander from work to our children, to what we are going to make for dinner or worse. We find ourselves in a tangled up web of ever-changing thoughts. That is why they call mindfulness and meditation a practice. It can take us a while to retrain our brains and begin to form new neural pathways that support mental calmness.

The second type of meditation is active meditation. You have probably already experienced active meditation in your life and did not even know it. Think about a time when you found yourself upset, distracted, or feeling ungrounded. Perhaps amid your drama, you went to the gym and had an intense workout. Your session ends, and as you leave the fitness center, you discover that you feel calm, clear, and remarkably invigorated. Yes, exercising can be a form of active meditation. The same is true for dancing, jogging, raking leaves, scrubbing a bathtub, or performing a ritual.

What matters is the intensity you employ as you pursue any of these activities. What you do is unimportant as long as your mind focuses on one thing and one thing only. You can practice mindful meditation anytime and anywhere. You can do it while you are brushing your teeth or washing the dishes, going for a walk, or reading a book. It is about keeping your attention on what is going on at that particular moment. Gently bring your mind back to the original focal point if you find it wandering. Be kind to yourself as you begin doing this. With a little time and practice, you will see immense changes occurring right before your eyes.

Simple Mindfulness Techniques

One simple mindfulness technique you can use is called the "ho'oponopono." The ho'oponopono is a Hawaiian meditative practice of reconciliation and forgiveness. It consists of four simple statements:

I'm sorry,

Please forgive me,

I love you,

Thank you.

The ho'oponopono is similar to an affirmation. This chant projects the energy of acceptance, grounding, and neutrality. Consider repeating the ho'oponopono if intrusive thoughts plague your life. Use it to shift your mind's focus away from your problems to one of healing.

Tied to this is breathing! Breathing is an excellent tool for calming both the nervous system and your overtaxed mind. It naturally puts your body into a calm state. Breathe fully as you repeat the ho'oponopono. Feel your body and mind shift with each breath you take, moving you from wherever you have been, back into the present moment.

Taking Inventory

Another way of supporting our inner transformation is by observing the dynamics of what is going on inside. Through it, you can start to unwind your psyche and heal your emotional wounding. This knowledge can help you identify what sets you off while providing you with the opportunity to make different choices, more mature choices when you encounter an uncomfortable situation. It also causes you to pause, check what is going on inside, and respond more skillfully. It gives you a chance to step out of your habitual patterns and view a situation from a more expanded perspective.

When you feel anxious, worried, or afraid, take a few deep breaths. This act will help to calm your body and quiet your mind. Remind yourself that these are just emotions triggered by your thoughts. It is natural to feel these things. Let them

Mindfulness

"be" without trying to manipulate or change the experience. Do not push them away, either. The more you struggle with them, the stronger they can become, and the more entangled you can get with them. Internalize questions such as:

- What are you trying to reveal to me?
- What just happened that stirred me up?
- Why am I feeling so anxious?
- What thoughts are rolling around in my mind that is disturbing my inner world?
- What concepts keep coming back, trying to fill my mental slot?
- What am I feeling in my body while all of this is going on?

Perhaps, the triggering situation is only sitting on the surface of something much more profound. Maybe what got activated is the pain from a wound that occurred in your distant past. Open yourself up to this possibility. Ask your intuition to revelation its origin and support you as you work to uncover the submerged trauma. Keep breathing as you work through this process.

Working With Worry

If worry is where your mind traditionally goes when challenging circumstances present themselves, then perhaps asking yourself some basic questions can resolve or at least lessen the fear you may be experiencing. Check-in and inquire, "*Is it that bad?*" "*What is the worst thing that could happen?*" "*What steps can I take to resolve this situation?*" Inquiries such as these support you as you begin to take control of what is going on inside. They help shift you from a place of helplessness to a proactive one, one in which you may feel like you are in control of your destiny.

Take A Worry Break

You might also want to try the strategy of postponing your negative thoughts. If you find yourself going in for another round of rumination or worry, give yourself permission to put them off until a later designated time. Tell yourself you do not need to think about it right now. You can go back and deal with these issues during a predetermined time, be it later in the day or even the following week. Sometimes just by putting it off, you can stop feeding your negative thoughts and the associated momentum. You may find that this technique can help you let go of what you were previously worrying about entirely.

Talk It Out

Sometimes it is a good idea to talk to someone about what you are thinking and feeling. It can provide you with the prospect of unraveling what may seem like a jumbled up confusing mess in your mind. It can also help you to delve deeper into your underlying issues rather than just dealing with them on surface levels. Whether you talk to a counselor or a good friend, the act of vocalized and expressing what is going on inside can be very healing.

Journaling

Journaling is another fantastic technique you can use to sort out your thoughts and make sense of what is going on inside. It can be especially useful if there is not anyone you can readily go to for support.

Journaling For Health And Well Being

Journaling is a way in which we can record what is going on in our lives. Almost anything you can get down onto a piece of paper can go into a journal. You can fill them with your ideas, facts, figures, photos, sketches, poetry, and quotes. In health and healing circles, when one speaks of journaling, it often implies the act of writing down our thoughts, ideas, feelings, and emotions. Many use it as a tool for personal growth and increased self-awareness. When utilized in this way, journaling allows us to explore below the surface of the conscious mind.

Journaling supports our thought processes. People journal to help clarify their feelings, gain insights into choices they need to make, or to hash out difficulties they are experiencing. Some use them as a means to solve a problem in which the answer is elusive. People also journal to release the emotional pain and trauma they may have had or are currently experiencing in their lives, while others may use it to explore the blessings they receive.

Journaling is also a form of meditation. It helps to quiet the mind and body through focused intention. Many health professionals recommend journaling for stress reduction, to help relieve anxiety, or to work through complicated feelings. The kinds of insights and epiphanies that come to the surface once you put pen to paper are always surprising.

This self-help tool is straightforward to do and even master. All you need is a pen and a piece of paper. You might want to use something that will keep your entries collected together, such as a spiral-bound notebook or a blank sketchbook. Many stores nowadays also carry a wide variety of readymade journals from which you can choose. They come in all shapes and sizes, lined and unlined, decorated and plain. This journal is yours and yours alone, so pick what appeals to you.

With your journal in hand, think of something to write about. Topics can be as simple as writing about your day, or you can use it to dig into the depths of why certain events trigger you. As you begin to write, do not just put down the facts, incorporate what you were thinking or how you were feeling about a situation, be it happy, sad, negative, or positive.

The stream of words coming to you, as you begin writing, may start slow, but as your mind and body begin to relax, and you commence accessing the information stored inside of you, your words will naturally start to flow. Allow one thought to lead to another and then another.

Sometimes your insights will want to come out very specifically in one fell swoop. At other times, they may twist and turn from one idea to the next. You might find that you will reach what feels like multiple branches your thoughts want to follow. This can occur when trying to work out a complex problem, where each branch represents an aspect of an issue that needs addressing. It is normal to have other questions, concerns, or thought tracks come to the surface. It is a part of the process. Jot a quick note to yourself on the top or side of your page and keep going. You can always come back to these topics later.

Do not worry about spelling or grammar while you write. Let your hand move quickly and freely across the page. If you think you have made a mistake or change your mind, leave it. Do not waste your time erasing or crossing out words and potentially interrupting your flow.

You know that you have neared the conclusion of a segment when your inner stream of thought has slowed down. You might have written one paragraph or ten pages. You can choose to stop writing at this point or move on to another branch that may have presented itself earlier.

If you have never journaled before, try it. It is the one tool you can utilize where no experience is required. You cannot hurt yourself or others as you process through your inner world, and best of all - spelling is optional. Be open to the healing aspects it can provide. Use it to help you access the innate wisdom you already possess. You will be amazed how much clearer everything can become once you have explored it in writing.

Letting Go And Letting God

There will come a time when it might be a good idea to consider forgiving the people in your life who have hurt you. Before we delve into this topic, understand... Forgiveness and forgiving those who have wronged you is not always easy to do. If it were easy, everyone would be doing it. Like addressing your fears, it requires you to take a deep breath and become a bigger person. Forgiveness, however, can transform your hurt into deep inner healing.

We make a conscious decision to let go of our anger, rage, and resentment toward another when we forgive. It can provide us with the opportunity to move on with our lives with an increased sense of freedom and inner peace and a lessening of the negative feelings often associated with painful memories.

Forgiveness transforms what you are experiencing in your inner world. Forgiveness will help reduce your sensitivity to triggering situations where you find yourself dwelling on painful memories. Without forgiveness, whenever a similar situation activates you, you are the one who suffers, not them.

When we are hurt, harmed, abused, or betrayed, the thought of forgiving the offender may seem out of the question. But holding onto the intense pain, corrosive anger, or the uncontrollable rage, you may feel inside can be even more harmful to your wellbeing than the original situation. The problem for many is: intellectually, we may want to forgive someone, but the resentment we feel in our hearts lingers.

Addressing Anger And Resentment

Resentment is often confused with anger, but they are not the same. Anger is a short-lived emotion that is natural and survival-oriented. Anger often starts as an aggravation, irritation, or frustration such as when someone unexpectedly pulls out in front of us on the freeway. Resentment, on the other hand, can be much more.

You can compare resentment to holding on to a burning ember with the intention of throwing it at someone else. Unfortunately, all we end up doing is burning ourselves. When we feel resentful, we experience the pain of our past over and over again. It takes a toll on our emotional well-being and can negatively affect our physical health as well.

Resentment works on the body and mind twenty-four hours a day. It can affect our heart by weakening our heart rate and increasing our blood pressure. It can disrupt our brain waves by affecting our ability to think clearly and make healthy decisions. It can distress our muscular-skeletal systems producing headaches, stomachaches, muscle and joint pain, dizziness, and feeling of fatigue. It can also depress our immune system leaving it harder for us to ward off disease. The amount of mental, emotional, and physical energy required to stuff feelings of resentment and keep them at bay is astronomical.

There is another massive implication that needs considering when talking about resentment. When we are resentful, we are giving individuals and situation power over us: power over our sleep, our appetites, our blood pressure, our health, and our happiness.

Coming to forgiveness may take a while. You have to honor your grief, acknowledge your outrage, accept your sadness, and recognize your loss. And yes, there will be times and situations that will set you off. These are the instances when it is most important to love and nurture yourself. You may find yourself trapped living in the dark, murky underpinnings of your own vindictive, bitter soul if you choose to hang on to your resentment. Do not let the pain of your past define who you are.

Please do not take this the wrong way! Forgiveness does not let the offender off the hook. Forgiving an abusive individual does not mean that you forget, suppress, gloss over, or deny the seriousness of what they have done. It does not mean that you condone their behavior or take away their accountability. And it especially does not mean that you should ignore your misery with a stiff upper lip.

There is a time to let go of our grudges and forgive. Forgiveness can provide a path to peace. It is an excellent way to help reconcile a relationship. Forgiveness, on the other hand, is not a tool the malefactor can or should use to manipulate and continue to harm you without impunity.

They transgress, and you forgive them. They transgress, you forgive. Despite how many times you may have granted your abusive partner forgiveness, their bad behavior continues amidst their begs, pleads, and promises to change. This forgiveness cycle may be why you found yourself repeatedly re-engaging in your unhealthy relationship. You forgave them with the hope of them changing, which never happened. Forgiveness does not mean you should or have to hang around for more maltreatment. You can still forgive someone regardless of whether they deserve it or not.

Forgiving Yourself

If you are having a hard time imagining forgiving someone else right now, maybe you can find it within your heart to forgive yourself. Self-forgiveness is all about looking at the mistakes you have made, owning them, and learning the lesson they provide with the goal of not repeating them. You may be asking yourself, "*Forgive myself? For what? I did not do anything wrong. They did this to me! How am I responsible for any of this?*"

The reality is, and this one may sting, especially if you are a victim of childhood neglect or abuse, you chose to believe the lies. You chose to interpret the things said, and the actions taken by others, as true. Then you fashioned your entire life around the lies. Your uninformed choice sits beneath your whole life experience and defines who you are, or at least who you were.

You did not deserve to be abused, violated, assaulted, or taken advantage of. Find compassion for yourself in this situation. Do not blame yourself for being deceived. Your parents created a false world, one you have been living in your whole life. They are guilty for their part, their massive part in it, but you have to take ownership and responsibility for your part as well. You can try to blame everyone involved, but blaming them will not change you into a different person. It will not fix what happened.

You were a child. You were ill-equipped to correctly decipher the validity of the core beliefs you took on, but bottom line, you did choose. And as with any choice, you have to accept the associated consequences that come with your choices. If you have found yourself burdened by recurring toxic relationships, this sadly is just one of the results of believing the lies.

Another part of forgiveness is about giving up all hope of having a different past, different parents, different life events, or different outcomes. You can move out of living in a victim, poor me mentality by accepting what happened. Congratulate yourself. Celebrate your victory. You survived. Learn from your adverse life experiences. Acknowledge the strengths you developed and then move on with the hope of a better, brighter future. Own your role as a Wounded Healer.

I Was Such A Fool

Then there is the shame. Society often invalidates our traumatic experiences and attempts to minimize the impact they have on our psyche. As adults, we end up feeling guilty and humiliated for something that was inflicted on us and was outside of our control. We are taught to internalize these feelings and are left believing we played a substantial role in what happened. We start blaming ourselves.

Shame, along with a harsh inner critic, can cause us to begin interrogating ourselves with invalidating questions such as *"How could I have gotten caught up in this in the first place?" "How could I have been so naïve?" "Why didn't I see what was going on sooner?"*

When we experience shame, we feel poorly about ourselves. It impacts our self-esteem and sense of self-worth. It makes us feel as if we need to apologize for or justify our actions or the behavior of those involved. We end up trying to explain away the entire situation so that we can "save face." If you stayed in a toxic relationship too long, own it. Do not beat yourself up for being sucked in by a predator. Even the best of us have been fooled by manipulative people who present a false image of who they are.

Our sense of shame has another devastating effect on our inner world. It causes us to conceal a part of ourselves. It forces us to hide our pain, our suffering, both of which are part of our life stories. It turns our history, both past, and present, into being a secret that is locked up behind heavy doors of silence. What happened to us, in civilized society, is just not discussed. We may also choose to hide our reality because we do not want to harm the perpetrator by exposing their misdeeds to the world.

Yet it happened. It is a part of you. By secreting the painful aspects of who you are, you are holding back your truth and are unable to be authentic to yourself much less anyone else. It can take an enormous amount of pressure off you when you come out about your history and acknowledge what occurred. You no longer have to live in a secretive world where your pain and suffering is locked up inside of you. Owning your truth, uncomfortable as it may be, is freeing.

Steps To Forgiveness

There are several ways in which you can begin to forgive those that have hurt you.

Finding Empathy

Finding empathy or compassion for your abuser can aid in the forgiveness process. In most instances, abusers were abused themselves. Their painful history does not justify their actions and behaviors, but do you honestly feel as if they purposefully set out to cause you pain. Try understanding what they were dealing with at the time. Were they going through a rough patch? Were they operating at a deficit? Were they suffering from inner wounds themselves? Sometimes understanding can lead to forgiveness.

Express How You Feel

Another key concept in finding it within your heart to forgive is being able to express how you feel. Letting the other person know how their actions affected you can help discharge the energy you have trapped inside. Expressing your inner pain can allow for some level of reconciliation. If, on the other hand, you have cut off the relationship or they are no longer in your life, try writing them a letter expressing yourself. Putting your feelings into words can help you in much the same way having a conversation does. You can burn or tear up the note when you have finished, which also supports the process of letting go.

Journal About Your Life History

You can also spend some time journaling about what happened. You can journal about the situation and how you were hurt or wronged. More importantly, journaling about what you gained from a negative experience provides added benefits, including an increased ability to forgive and move on. You can also use this tool to reframe your story from one of being a victim to one of increased strength.

Develop An Attitude Of Gratitude

You can also choose to shift your focus from all of the bad things that have happened (victim mentality) and view the same situation from a place of gratitude. Gratitude is an emotion conveying appreciation for what one has or receives. When you express gratitude, you take the time to notice and reflect upon the goodness in your life. It refocuses the mind from a state of lack, or that your needs will not be met, to a place of feeling happy and satisfied. It allows you to celebrate the present while replacing negative emotions that can interfere with your enjoyment of life.

Studies put forward that expressing gratitude is consistently tied to greater happiness. What many of us remember are the hurtful things that have happened to us. We end up feeling sad, unhappy, or depressed when we spend all of our time thinking about adverse situations. Gratitude does not make you happier, according to gratitude researcher Robert Emmons, it is happiness itself! It causes you to focus on and relish your positive experiences. It can be used to turn bad things into good because it reminds you of what is important.

New positive neural pathways form when we express gratitude, which can impact how we perceive life. It triggers a positive feedback loop. Gratitude makes us feel more grateful. Studies indicate that being grateful increases energy levels. It reduces anxiety, feelings of disappointment, and helps us bounce back from stressful situations quicker. It can leave you feeling more alive, with increased joy, pleasure, and optimism, in your day to day existence. Being grateful for all life hands you, increases your self-esteem and overall levels of positive emotions.

To educate yourself for the feeling of gratitude means to take nothing for granted, but to always seek out and value the kindness that will stand behind the action. Nothing that is done for you is a matter of course. Everything originates in a will for the good, which is directed at you. Train yourself never to put off the word or action for the expression of gratitude.

-- Albert Schweitzer

You can also apply gratitude to your past to help you retrieve positive memories. It allows you to re-remember your history and view it from a new perspective, with a focus on what you gained and not what you lost. For example, it can be used to revisit elements from your childhood and reframe them.

Who would you be today if you had not had your life experiences? Be grateful for the person you became, for your ability to survive challenges situations. Each of them caused you to grow into the unique vital individual you are today. When you re-contextualize your past, you will never be the victim of your upbringing again.

What can you be grateful for? Everything and anything. Sure, you can be thankful for the new job, the up-close parking spot, or the great buy you got at the store, but the best way to benefit from an attitude of gratitude is to find new things to be grateful for every day.

Be grateful for the roof over your head and the food you have to eat. Be grateful when you have the opportunity to learn something new or for the difficult things you encounter that cause you to grow. Be grateful for the challenges that help you to build strength and character. It is easy to be thankful for the good things in life, but also be grateful for the setback as well. You can turn an initial negative perception into the positive by finding the blessing in it. Count your blessings, even in the worst of times, with gratitude.

There are several ways to elicit an attitude of gratitude.

Gratitude Journal

People who want to have more happiness in their lives will often work with a gratitude journal. In it, they will write down the gifts they receive.

Pick a time every day or every week and reflect on your life. What went right? What transpired that made you happy or left you feeling satisfied? If you experienced challenges, stop complaining about what occurred. Mentally flip the switch and focus on what positives came out if it. Find the silver lining. What did you learn about yourself or from the situation? Take the time regularly to acknowledge all the good you have encountered.

Find A Gratitude Partner

Another way to practice gratitude is to share it with a friend or partner. Get into the daily practice of discussing what you are grateful for. Ask each other questions, such as *"What made you happy today?"* or *"What blessings did you encounter?"* Do not let the conversation become about all of the bad things that happened to you that day. Support each other by raising each other's awareness to negative thinking. This act will encourage you to make a mental shift from pessimistic thoughts to ones of joy.

In all that you do, say thank you to yourself, your friends, your family and your life situations, good or bad. This is the essence of gratitude.

Energy Medicine

So far, we have explored how you can bring about changes in your life by addressing your negative thoughts and triggered reactions to troubling situations. But we are more than just a physical body, and healing can also be facilitated by working on subtle energy levels. As we explored in the chapter *Beyond The Physical Body*, we are made up of a number of elements that exist on subtle energy planes, each of which plays a role in our ability to be whole and experience life in the present moment. These parts include the aura, the chakras, the subtle energy channels, the nadis, and the universal life force energy that flows through our bodies.

Our aura and chakras respond to and record all of our life experiences. The aura holds onto the energy of our unprocessed thoughts and emotions. It is this energy, these "pictures" that get activated when we are triggered. The chakras open up to or shut down to the flow of subtle energy, depending on the circumstances encountered. If we experience adversity in which we want to protect ourselves, our chakras will reduce the amount of energy and information coming into our internal environment. This reaction is most easily recognized when we encounter something that scares us. The terror we feel reduces the aperture of our first chakra, which activates our fight or flight mechanism.

Our chakras can also open up if we are seeking to bring in additional information from the world around us. It can leave us more sensitive to our environment and is one reason why so many individuals who were brought up in a home of abuse or neglect find themselves empathic. Their desire to sense even the smallest tidbit of nurturing, or know when to duck and cover when the energy has shifted for the worst, has opened up their chakras to receiving increased stimuli. This increase in information allows them to react appropriately to the situation.

When our subtle energy system is balanced, we can perform at our optimal physical, mental, and emotional potential. When it is imbalanced, we often experience problems. These imbalances can affect every facet of our lives.

Your life force energy is like a fast-moving stream. Imagine each trauma you have experienced as a large stone. These stones are placed in your stream. Each stone causes your energy to deviate its path, slowing down its forward movement, as it goes around the obstruction. If one of your early life experiences vibrated at the frequency of invalidation, the effect on the flow of your life force energy might not be very significant. If, however, you repeatedly felt invalidated, your stream might soon find itself filled with stones.

These impediments grow instance by instance, cycle by cycle, stone after stone, until the body and psyche starts to manifest issues. These can include fear, narrow-mindedness, disrespect for life and nature, materialism, anger, rage, phobias, depression, hate, frustration, anxiety, and even as physical disease.

Imbalances to our subtle energy system can inhibit our ability to experience the world clearly because there is too much "stuff" interfering with the natural movement of our subtle energy. It acts as a negative filter on our internal world and world view. These obstructions are reminiscent of the barnacle-encrusted self-worth diamond that resides in our fourth chakra, our heart center. The stones of our internal traumas interfere with our ability to experience the beauty of who we are and of life in general.

Energy medicine techniques can help to restore the movement of your subtle life force energy. Meditation, mindfulness, and guided imagery are all forms of energy medicine. Countless other tools can be employed to affect it, as well.

The goal of energy medicine is to restore balance and harmony to all the parts of our being. It helps to get our life force energy flowing again by clearing the energetic pathways between the chakras. It also raises the vibratory level of our auric field, which holds our negative thoughts and emotions, causing them to dissolve and fade away.

Anyone can perform energy medicine on themselves. You are not limited to experiencing its healing effects when working with a licensed practitioner. The key to successfully working with energy medicine is the power of your intention.

Lynne McTaggart and other new thought authors state that intention is a vital part of healing and underlies the effectiveness of energy medicine. In one study with HIV patients, it was found that regardless of the type of therapy performed, shamanistic, reiki, quantum touch, the researchers discovered that it was not the modality that made the difference. It was the level of focus and intention the practitioner used when performing the work.

If your intention is not applied, you can pray, smudge and say affirmations until the cows come home, but more than likely, nothing will happen. You have to see it, feel it, and want it from the depth of your being. You have to fill your one empty mental slot with it and be fully in the process for it to work effectively.

We will be exploring several techniques that can be used to affect the body's energetic systems positively. Our survey begins with traditional cleansing methods, which have been practiced by all known cultures and religious groups on the Earth.

Ritual Purification

The ancient practice of ritual purification can take on many forms. It has been used, historically speaking, to remove specifically defined "uncleanliness" and reestablish one's purity. There are several items that traditional cultures employed as vehicles for cleanliness. They include water, smoke, and fire.

Indigenous people around the world have utilized the beneficial healing properties smoke and fire offer for thousands of years. One need only think of the incense burned in churches and temples. Its purpose is to sanctify a space. The practice of employing smoke for personal healing has only come into Western consciousness recently. It was adopted from Amerindian culture and is called "smudging." Smudging (the name given to the sacred smoke bowl blessing) was used to cleanse a person's body, mind, and spirit before a holy ceremony.

Today, the ritual of smudging can be found in many energy healers' arsenal, where it is used to remove negative energy, aka "bad mojo," from people, places, and objects that might be compromising your world. You can smudge yourself, your home, and anything that belongs to you. If you have recently ended a toxic relationship, then perhaps smudging yourself and your environment will help begin the healing process.

You can use a variety of dried herbs when smudging. The most familiar one is dried sage. It is used to remove the vibration of outside or unwanted influences. Its smoke is said to cleanse, bless, and heal a person or object. Sweetgrass can be employed to purify your space, while juniper berry can promote purification and protection. Utilizing cedar brings in increased positive energy and emotions, while palo santo blesses, heals, and consecrates a person or location.

These herbs can be used individually or combined for an increased synergistic effect. Smudging herbs can be purchased separately or in the form of a smudge stick, where a variety of smudging herbs are combined. Having a heatproof dish handy is recommended before you begin smudging. Since you will be igniting the herbs, having somewhere to put their burning ashes is prudent.

Remember, the most critical component of smudging is not the herbs you use but the intention and focus you apply to the process. Rituals, such as smudging, are designed to help increase your focus while clarifying your intentions.

The Smudging Ritual

Light a couple of herb pieces, or the end of your smudge stick, and allow it to catch fire. Let it burn for several seconds. Gently blow on it until your smudge begins to glow and smoke but is no longer on fire. Place these materials into your heatproof dish. A little goes a long way when working with dried herbs. They can produce a lot of smoke, so do not go overboard thinking more is better. You do not want your neighbors to wonder if your house is on fire.

Fan the smoke, using your hand or a feather, over and around your body. Imagine, as the smoke climbs, that whatever it may be, whatever negative energy it may encounter is effortlessly cleared. Some believe that our prayers (intentions) will rise to the world of spirit to be seen, heard, and acted on. Watch as discordant vibrations rise with the smoke. Breathe deeply as you work through this process. Continue to smudge yourself until you feel a shift in your inner world. You can end the clearing here, or you can continue and purify your environment.

Move around your house, fanning the smoke throughout the space. Travel from room to room, cleansing them. Smudge inside the closets or anything that could use their vibrations raised. Pay special attention to any items that may trigger uncomfortable memories for you.

Smudging can be especially valuable when ending a relationship. It can help to break the energetic ties between you and your former partner and help to dissolve the emotional charge the memories may have for you. It can also help eliminate any residual personal energy of your ex-lover, which has stagnated in your home.

Extinguish your smudge when you are done or let it burn out on its own. Some contend that if it is left to burn out on its own, the herbs will burn as long and as strong as it needs to fulfill the intention you set. Take a nice deep breath and notice how you feel. Most people comment that they feel more grounded, more centered, or lighter. You can smudge whenever you want and as often as you need to support your healing.

The same technique can be done in a pinch with a piece of your favorite incense if smudging materials are not available.

Spring Cleaning

Another way of clearing the energy of your house is to do a "spring cleaning." Remember spring cleaning? It is where you go through your home and scrub it from top to bottom. Yes, you heard me right, clean out your closets, dust, move the furniture around, and wash the windows. Get rid of things that you are not using anymore, and if you find any of your old flame's possessions, toss them out as well. They can hold on to the energy of their owner and is just one less thing to trigger painful memories. It will also help to reduce any ties you may have with them.

As you lighten the load in your home, the energy within it will also begin to clear. Moreover, while you may only think of spring-cleaning as the weather turns nice, it is a fabulous way to get the energy moving in your home again. You not only end up with a beautiful spotless house, but you will also experience a lighter, cleaner fresher feeling in and around you.

Healing With Water

Another incredible technique you can use to spruce up the energy in your abode is to clear it with water. Water, like fire and smoke, is a tool our ancestors used for ritual purification. We can all recognize the cleaning and restorative properties water has. The technique is similar to smudging, but the only supplies you need for this method is some water and something to put it in. A new spray bottle, one free of cleaning products, works best.

Crystals or essential oils can be added to the water. You can even say a blessing over it before you use it. Do what feels right to you. No matter what you choose, it will support your intentions and amplify the healing process.

Imagine there is a giant drain in the center of the room as you begin. Envision any water you spray into the room washing away any negative energy it encounters down the drain you just created. Start in the corner of one room, spraying water from your sprits bottle towards the ceiling. Work your way around each wall and then begin to spiral around the room, still misting, until you come to the center. Watch as the water cleanses out any unwanted vibrations. Move onto the next room when the one you are working on feels complete.

Sometimes items in our home, like a sofa or bookcase, might also need to be cleared, and this technique works exceptionally well to revitalize them. Take a few deep breaths and walk from room to room when complete. Notice how your house now feels to you.

Energetic Protection

Once you have your house cleaner and fresher feeling, it is also a good idea to protect it from outside influences. There are a handful of things you can use to do this. First, let us start with a simple visualization. To protect your space, you can create an energetic bubble around it. You can imagine it like a giant soap bubble around your entire house or apartment. If you share space with other people, imagine it enveloping YOUR space and not everyone's. As you envision this in your mind's eye, set the intention, "*I am surrounding myself with a protective bubble that will help to keep me safe and secure.*"

Another technique you can employ to protect your home is to create a protection grid. To do this, you will need a minimum of four crystals. The best crystals to use for this method are obsidian, amethyst, or clear quartz.

Obsidian

Obsidian can help you dispel harmful energies. It can be used to shield you and your environment from unwanted influence and protect you from the detrimental effects of friends, family, neighbors, or any ghostly presence that may be affecting you. Obsidian also guards against psychic attack. It helps to break up energy blockages, especially in those who are unable or unwilling to let go of the past. Its healing ability can help to eliminate negative emotions such as anger, jealousy, fear, and resentment. You can set your intention by internalizing, "*This healing stone will protect and clear my environment from negative energies.*"

Amethyst

The powerful and protective qualities of amethyst can help to transform lower vibrations into higher ones. It can be used to change the negative energy you may be experiencing in your home. The natural calming properties and strong healing powers of this stone can help to relieve stress and soothe irritability. It functions to dissolve feelings of sadness and grief while encouraging and promoting inner strength. It can also be employed to dispel feelings of rage, anger, fear, and anxiety and support a state of peace and tranquility. You can set the intention for amethyst by stating, "*This healing stone will transform any lower or negative energy vibrations into ones of love and light.*"

Clear Quartz

Clear quartz can support all of your healing and protection work. You can use it alone or in conjunction with any other healing stone. Clear quarts allows you to set your own healing intentions and works to augment the power of them. This stone is very programmable and will hold your objective for extended periods. You can set whatever purpose you want with clear quartz. You might use a statement such as "*This healing stone will* _____ *(fill in your intention here)* _____."

To create your protection grid, place one crystal into the four corners of your home. It is time to create a grid of energy in your mind's eyes once they are in place. Have the crystal in one corner connect energetically to the one in the next until you have created a square around your space. Next, imagine four energetic lines extending upward along the walls of your home.

Follow the walls up in each corner until you have reached the height of your home. Then connect each corner until you have a giant square or rectangle. For those interested, you can create a pyramid by combining the upper points of the grid up over the center of your home. Again, create an intention such as, "*I am surrounding myself with a grid of protection that will help to keep me safe and secure in the coming year.*"

Grounding

Another simple energy medicine technique is grounding. When we ground, we work to restore the movement of energy through our entire body, starting at the top of the head at the seventh chakra down to the base of the spine, where our first chakra resides.

Grounding, or being grounded, implies a feeling of

stability, certainty, clarity, and strength. We often use this term when describing someone who is secure, confident, yet yielding and has a down-to-earth quality. Grounding brings us, as spirit, back into our bodies here on the physical plane. It also supports the movement of subtle lifeforce energy through the subtle bodies and chakras. We often experience an increased sense of clarity, balance, and the ability to be in the present moment when we are grounded.

We all have grounding cords through which we anchor ourselves, our physical and subtle bodies into the earth. It is part of our subtle energy system, and technically speaking, it is another word for the nadis that extends out of our first chakra. Some people's nadis are long, some are short, some release mental and emotional energy efficiently, others not as well. It is through our grounding cord that we can reconnect with the Earth and release discordant energy. If we are not adequately grounding, we often have a hard time letting go.

Let us look at grounding in a different way. In electrical terms, objects with an excess of charge, either positive or negative, can have this charge removed by a process known as grounding. We have all experienced a discharge of electric energy when we get shocked after walking across a carpet and then touching a metal doorknob. The instantaneous release of built-up static electricity caused the shock.

A lightning rod is a classic example of a ground. When lightning hits a lightning rod, the charge follows along a wire that is firmly planted within the earth. The wire creates a conducting pathway for the electrically charged lightning, where it is dissipated. Our grounding cords work much in the same way.

Grounding is a great way to revive our energy as well as prepare ourselves for meditation. It is especially useful in liberating us from things that disturb our internal world. It serves as a vehicle to release stagnant or surplus emotional energy from our bodies. If you find yourself triggered by a life event, in a cycle of worry or rumination, grounding is an excellent way to help calm the mind and sooth the spirit.

We can all create new grounding cords for ourselves. All you need do is visualize a line of energy connecting your first chakra, the energy center located at the base of your spine, to the center of the planet. As you imagine it in your mind's eye, hold the intention that it will help you to release any unwanted or surplus energy from your body and subtle energy system. The exercise below will help you to experience what it feels like to be grounded.

- *To begin, take a nice deep breath.*
- *Take a moment to notice what is happening around you.*
- *Orient yourself to your surroundings.*
- *Take another deep breath and say hello to your body.*
- *Pause and listen to your heartbeat.*
- *Feel your chest rise and fall with each breath you take.*
- *Breathe in again, and allow yourself, as spirit, to effortlessly rest back into your body.*
- *This may take a few seconds, so be patient.*
- *As you continue breathing, allow yourself to relax even more.*

- *Take one more nice deep breath and let us begin creating a new grounding cord.*
- *Again, a grounding cord is a line of energy that runs from the first chakra, at the base of your spine, down to the center of the planet.*
- *Put your attention on your first chakra.*
- *You may notice it tingling, vibrating, or feeling warmer as you concentrate on this area of your body.*
- *Imagine that you can shake off your old grounding cord.*
- *Watch as gravity takes over, and your grounding cord falls to the center of the Earth.*
- *Give yourself a second to pause and take a few additional breaths.*
- *Now, in your mind's eye, visualize the center of the planet.*
- *The center of the planet can look any way you want. It can appear as a hollow ball or a solid sphere. It can be made of molten rock or like the insides of a baseball. It can even appear as a ball of light.*
- *Whatever you want the center of the planet to look like, have that appear in your mind's eye.*
- *When you are ready, create a line of energy from your first chakra, to the center of the planet.*
- *Have it appear as a hollow tube, like the one you might find extending out of your bathtub drain.*
- *Allow your new grounding cord to form easily and effortlessly.*
- *When it reaches the center of the planet, have it connect you firmly into its core.*

- *Congratulate yourself for having created a new grounding cord.*
- *Take another few deep breaths.*
- *Now it is time to set the intention.*
- *Ask your body to release any unwanted or discordant energy down your grounding cord in the same way water flows down the drain in your bathtub.*
- *Have it travel down your grounding cord to the center of the Earth.*
- *Take a moment to pause and breathe.*
- *Give your body a chance to let go.*
- *You might feel as your body begins to discharge, as if something is draining out of you or as if the anxiety or tension you were carrying has somehow magically disappeared.*
- *Perhaps you feel as if you have finally taken a weight off your shoulders?*
- *Maybe what you were previously experiencing has lessened or gone away completely.*
- *Notice how releasing energy feels to your body.*
- *Have you noticed any shifts in your energy?*
- *Do you feel more relaxed, centered, or clearer?*
- *Are you more at ease?*
- *This is the power of grounding at work.*
- *Continue to release down your grounding.*
- *Give this process a little time to work.*
- *Love yourself for a moment and give yourself and your body permission to let go of even more.*
- *Give this as much time as it needs.*

- When the flow of energy down your grounding cord slows down or when you feel complete, bring your attention back to the room.
- Take one final deep breath as you look around and reorient yourself to your surroundings.
- Enjoy the relaxation that grounding your body offers.

Interacting With Your Aura

Have you ever felt your aura? If you have not, it is super fun and easy to do. First, rub your hands together briskly. When you are ready, with your palms facing one another, hold your hands about four feet apart. Slowly bring them together.

Do you feel any tingling, pressure, or resistance in the palms of your hands? When you do, stop moving your hands and tune into the sensation. The sensation you are feeling is your aura! What does it feel like? Is it vibrant, hot, tingly, hard, soft, wispy, or delicate?

Continue bringing your hands closer together until they are about six to eight inches apart. Slowly move your hands in and out. Do you sense your hands being repelled by one another? Perhaps it feels like there is a ball of energy sitting between them?

Give this exercise a chance if you are not feeling your aura on the first try. It is no wonder why we refer to items such as our auric field as "subtle" energy. They have a soft or slight feel and can be difficult to initially detect, but once found, you will never be able to forget the experience.

Aura Fluffing

Now that you have felt and detected your auric field let us take it one step further and perform an energy medicine technique on it. We hold on to mental and emotional energies in our auric field. We clear it by sending the discordant energy down our grounding cord. The process can be like cleaning the windshield of our cars. We often do not realize how dirty our windshields are until we clean off the dust, dirt, and debris that has built up on it. The same thing happens with our aura, where we accumulate energy that is not serving us.

An aura fluff can help you release any energy you may be carrying around in your personal space. This tool can be used any time you want but is an excellent technique to employ at the end of a stressful day to clean off anything negative you may have picked up. It is refreshing and revitalizing. It can also be a lifesaver when one of our wounds gets triggered.

- To begin, drop your old grounding cord down to the center of the planet and create a new one.

- Set your intention and have your grounding cord release any unwanted mental and emotional energy from your body.
- Take a moment and let your grounding do its work.
- Now, take a nice deep breath.
- This is where the fun begins.
- Hold your right or left hand up in front of you.
- Make sure that your fingers are open, and your palm is facing away from you.
- Imagine you can see a squeegee, like the kind you would use to clean your car's windshield out in front of you.
- Grasp it in your extended hand.
- Move your hand around and observe how tangible the squeegee feels.
- Your squeegee is an intuitive tool. You are going to utilize it to clean your aura.
- You created this tool by using your intention.
- Imagine your aura as a giant glass bubble that surrounds you.
- Holding the squeegee with the rubber facing away from you, spray the inside of your auric bubble with window cleaner.
- Starting at the top of your head, at the seventh chakra, and going down to the ground, use your squeegee to wipe down the inside of your aura.
- Watch as any dirt or debris flows down its sides and down your grounding cord.
- Do you notice any roughness in your aura as you worked your way around your body?

- *Roughness in the aura indicates where energy has stagnated or become trapped in your auric field.*
- *Say hello to it and let it go.*
- *Work your way around your body, allowing all that has built up to be released.*
- *Do not forget to wipe down the area behind your back and around your feet.*
- *Pause and notice how good it feels to have your aura cleared of discordant energy when complete.*
- *Do you feel as if you have more room to be yourself?*
- *Do you feel clearer? More present?*
- *Now let us take an opportunity to replace some of the energy you have just moved out of your aura by filling it in with some of your own.*
- *You can do this by visualizing a soap bubble or a big water balloon over your head.*
- *Have it appear as a ball of golden white light.*
- *As you call back your energy, this ball of golden white light is going to get bigger and bigger as it fills up with more and more of your energy.*
- *Where did you leave your energy today?*
- *Is it still in your car?*
- *Or did you leave some of it at home?*
- *Is it with a child or spouse who has something for you to do?*
- *Or in a project at work? We often leave some of our life force energy in our jobs.*
- *Maybe you went to the grocery store or the bank?*
- *Think about where you left your energy and summon it back to you.*

- *Permit yourself to not know where you left it and summon that back too.*
- *Do this by drawing it in like a magnet. Allow your energy to drift into that water balloon, flowing into it and filling it up.*
- *Go ahead and watch.*
- *Notice how big that ball of energy gets.*
- *Look at how much energy you have left out in the world.*
- *Think about how good it is going to feel when you get to have it back.*
- *When the ball of golden white light is nice and big, and you are ready to fill yourself up, go ahead and poke a hole in it.*
- *Let your energy cascade over you.*
- *You might find it flowing onto you like water, like that water balloon just popped or a magnet just released.*
- *Have the energy you have just collected to stream into your aura.*
- *Have it refill and recharge you as it surrounds your body and penetrates your skin.*
- *Allow some of it to flow into your seventh chakra, through your body, and down your grounding cord.*
- *Notice how good this feels to your body as you give to yourself in this loving way.*
- *Take a deep breath.*
- *When your body feels full, vital, and refreshed, stretch it out and enjoy the blessings that an aura healing can provide.*

Deprogramming

"Conditioning," describes any involuntary or automatic response to an external stimulus. Conditioning always sits beneath any of the triggers we may experience. Conditioning is what happens when we associate two things together in a cause and effect relationship. Pavlov, for example, is best known for his work with dogs where he conditioned them to drool at the sound of a bell. Like Pavlov's animals, our conditioning can provoke a reaction in us.

As soon as we are born, we begin to create a vocabulary of behaviors where we learn to respond either positively or negatively to our experiences. We are taught to interpret life events in a particular way. Some events we may see as being tragic; others, we may celebrate. For example, when stricken with a terminal illness, some people see it as dreadful and go into a deep depression, while others take it as a challenge to overcome their illness or as a wakeup call to reevaluate their priorities in life. All of our likes, dislikes, preferences, and biases, which serve to define our personality, develop based upon conditioning.

Conditioning, especially negative emotional conditioning, can be self-perpetuating. The reality is, a life event has no meaning by itself, but only the meaning we assign to it. It is our interpretation of an incident that charges it, thus producing a negative or positive reaction. Negative conditioning often comes from the trauma we experience in our lives. Our dysfunctional life patterns reinforce it. It can leave us stuck in a prolonged negative emotional state. It is the well-worn path and is what forms our neural pathways.

Interestingly, conditioning (especially negative emotional conditioning) expresses itself as stagnant energy in our subtle energy system. Techniques, such as deprogramming, can help you break free of the limiting patterns that keep you experiencing unwanted mental and emotional states over and over again. It works by identifying where specific conditioned responses reside in the energetic body and clearing them.

Deprogramming is a simple technique to master. To deprogram yourself, you must first select an item, issue, or topic to evaluate and clear. You will also get to play with some magic purple dust. It will help you locate where your trapped negative conditioning is.

To deprogram yourself, you will be imaging you are sitting in a chair across from you. Place a chair directly across from where you will be working to experience its full effect. This request might sound a bit bizarre, but as you will soon discover, it assists in creating a deeper level of intention. Some people will also place a doll or stuffed animal in the chair across from them to aid in the intention process.

- *To begin, take a deep breath and give yourself a new grounding cord.*
- *Take a moment to clean out your auric field.*

- *In your mind's eye, pretend you can see yourself sitting in the chair facing you.*
- *When you are ready, select an issue or behavior that you would like to clear from the list below.*
- *Now it is time to have a bit of fun.*
- *Imagine you have a handful of magic purple dust.*
- *Toss the purple dust onto yourself with the intention that it will stick to the energy of the issue you selected and turn black when and where the problem is detected.*
- *Watch as the magic purple dust lands on your aura, your physical body, and your chakras.*
- *Observe it as it changes color from purple to black in the areas where this energy is trapped.*
- *Has the now black dust accumulated in one area more than another?*
- *Using your hand, a feather duster, a squeegee, a vacuum cleaner, or any other intuitive tool you can think of, remove the black dust from your body.*
- *Pay attention to how it feels to have this energy eliminated.*
- *Once all of the dust is gone, repeat the procedure.*
- *Keep doing this until the magic purple dust no longer adheres to your body or aura.*
- *Do not forget to toss some onto your back and the back of your aura.*
- *Take a nice deep breath when done and call back some of your energy into another giant ball of golden-white light.*
- *Have it fill your body and revitalize your spirit.*

Deprogramming List

Disappointment – Where do you hold on to the feeling of being let down?

Fear – Where do you lack security?

Guilt – Where do you hold on to sorrow, regret, or shame?

Invalidation – Where does your inner critic reside?

Neediness – Where do you need nurturing and love?

Pain – Where does physical or emotional pain rest in your body?

Pride – Where do you cling on to your personality or ego?

Prohibition – Where do you limit or invalidate yourself, which interferes with your ability to act?

Resentment – Where do you hold on to anger and resentment?

Resistance – Where do you hold onto energy that is not for your highest good?

As you become comfortable with this technique, there is no limit to what energies and emotions you can evaluate and eliminate from your personal space and your life.

Healing With Flower Power

Flower essences, or flower remedies, while not a hands-on energy medicine technique, are designed to harmonize our mental, emotional, and energetic bodies and support energy movement in the subtle energy system. Flower essences balance negative states of mind, such as anger, resentment, insecurity, or fear. They are very effective in helping us to recognize and rid ourselves of limiting or destructive patterns of behavior, resolve old traumas, and deal with painful emotions.

British physician Edward Bach, M.D., introduced flower remedies to the world in the 1930s. They are the vibrational imprint of living flowers that has been transferred and stabilized in water. They are made from the flowering part of a plant but are not aromatic like aromatherapy oils.

Bach developed what he called a "theory of types." The types are broken up into seven groups. They include fear, uncertainty, loneliness, oversensitivity, lack of interest in present circumstances, despondency, and over-concern for others. Based upon these types, Dr. Bach devised 38 wildflower essences for treatment for these negative moods and emotions. It is like deprogramming except in a bottle.

It is not necessary to believe in flower essences or any energy medicine technique to experience their beneficial effects. Unlike traditional medications, the way to recognize if a flower essence is working is to check-in and observe your inner world. If your inner world is feeling better, calmer, or more grounded than you might attribute these changes to the remedies.

Flower Essences operate similar to homeopathic remedies. When working with a homeopathic remedy, the general philosophy is not about how much you take at a time, but how frequently you utilize them. These remedies come in a liquid form and are traditionally distributed in small dropper bottles.

To take it, you shake the bottle gently and place a few drops under your tongue several times during the day. Typically, you take four drops of a specific flower essence at a time, which you repeat four times a day, or as needed. Use it more often throughout the day instead of increasing the number of drops for the best results.

You can also add four drops to a glass of water. You should also repeat this four times a day or as needed. At times, you might need to mix two or more remedies to match your precise mix of emotions. It is quite usual to take up to six or seven flower essences at the same time.

Typically there is no problem with taking flower remedies alongside other medicines. The active ingredient in a flower remedy is plant energy and not a physical substance. This trait means it will not interfere with the action of other medications, nor will the other medications stop the remedy from working. The only point of caution concerns the alcohol used to bottle and preserve the flower essences.

The original 38 traditional Bach flower essences and their application are listed below. You can work with one or pick up to six different remedies that you feel will help you with your healing. Use them as recommended. If you look online, you will see that Dr. Bach's followers have since added additional flower essence remedies. The same guidelines apply if you choose to work with any of them.

Bach Flower Essences include:

Agrimony - mental torture behind a cheerful face

Aspen - fear of unknown things

Beech - intolerance

Centaury - the inability to say 'No'

Cerato - lack of trust in one's own decisions

Cherry Plum - fear of the mind giving way

Chestnut Bud - failure to learn from mistakes

Chicory - selfish, possessive love

Clematis - dreaming of the future without working in the present

Crab Apple - the cleansing remedy, also for self-hatred

Elm - overwhelmed by responsibility

Gentian - discouragement after a setback

Gorse - hopelessness and despair

Heather - self-centeredness and self-concern

Holly - hatred, envy, and jealousy

Honeysuckle - living in the past

Hornbeam - tiredness at the thought of doing something

Impatiens - impatience

Larch - lack of confidence

Mimulus - fear of known things

Mustard - deep gloom for no reason

Oak - the plodder who keeps going past the point of exhaustion

Olive - exhaustion following mental or physical effort

Pine - guilt

Red Chestnut - over-concern for the welfare of loved ones

Rock Rose - terror and fright

Rock Water - self-denial, rigidity, and self-repression

Scleranthus - inability to choose between alternatives

Sweet Chestnut - Extreme mental anguish, when everything has been tried, and there is no light left

Vervain - over-enthusiasm

Vine - dominance and inflexibility

Walnut - protection from change and unwanted influences

Water Violet - quiet self-reliance leading to isolation

White Chestnut - unwanted thoughts and mental arguments

Wild Oat - uncertainty over one's direction in life

Wild Rose - drifting, resignation, apathy

Willow - self-pity and resentment

Rescue Remedy - emotional first-aid kit

For more information about the Bach Flower Essence formulations, please visit https://www.bachcentre.com/

Cutting The Cords That Bind Us
How Energy Cords Effect Us

Cords are an interesting and complex phenomenon that occurs on subtle levels. The effect of these invisible structures can be intense and far-reaching. There have been several places earlier in the text where we could have broached the concept of energetic cords. It seemed essential to save all of this subtle energy goodness for one spot and cover it as a whole. Now it is time to dig in. You have enough background regarding subtle energy to better understand what we will be discussing.

Energy cords play a crucial role when talking about our personal, professional or romantic encounters. They are why, at the beginning of a relationship, we cannot get our new special someone off our minds. We feel energized and excited. As the relationship deepens and we come closer to the other person, the emotional connection becomes stronger. This increased connection occurs because the cords between you and your new friend have become larger and more defined.

Cords can also leave you wondering why you cannot stop thinking about your former boyfriend or girlfriend, husband or wife, once the relationship has ended. You might find yourself reliving all of the gory details, spending countless hours trying to understand what just happened or ruminating about all of the harmful and hurtful things they did to you. You might also find yourself, regardless of what you do, unable to get them out of your head? Why? Because you may still have intact energetic cords connecting you to your former lover.

Cords exist on the subtle energy plane in the same way your aura and chakras do. The difference between the components that make up your subtle body and cords is that cords are not part of your subtle anatomy. Unlike a chakra, a cord is an energetic creation between two points. You created a cord, for example, when you experienced grounding earlier. A grounding cord, by definition, is a line of energy that connects your first chakra to the center of the planet.

Energy cords help us to relate to one another on non-verbal levels. They are an integral part of the human experience and are essential to our survival. They form naturally and unintentionally whenever we interact with another person. We can be physically close to someone, or we can be thousands of miles away. Cords exist outside of time and space. Distance plays no role in their formation.

Cords are like talking on the telephone. When you make a call or receive one, a connection is established between you and the other party. Energy cords can form between friends, lovers, workmates, and even people we despise. They can vary in size from being thread-like in diameter to becoming as large as a plumbing pipe. The dimensions differ depending on the depth and breadth of our connection. The bigger a cord is the easier and faster information is exchanged.

Cords often connect to our chakras, but we can cord or be corded anywhere on our bodies. We create energetic cords when we think about, talk about, or interact with someone. Anywhere we put our focus and attention, they can materialize. Likewise, if someone is thinking about us, or focusing on us, they can connect to us via a cord. Energy cords are one reason why we can become emotionally attached to someone we barely know, like the rude waitress we find ourselves obsessed with.

On some levels, cords are like a cat's whiskers where they help keep us apprised of what is going on. They can offer two individuals in-depth and potentially critical information. We have all heard stories of people sensing that something may have happened to their spouse, parent, or child long before the phone rings. And while there might be a bit of psychic ability involved, more often than not, the receiver has picked up on the information being passed along on the energy cords that connect them. The receiving individual might not know precisely what is going on, but for some reason, unbeknownst to them, they may start anxiously thinking about the other person.

Cords are also the reason why a mother will wake up out of a dead sleep the second her newborn stirs. Information from the child was transmitted along the cord, letting the new mother know he or she is awake.

Energy cords, unfortunately, are not always positive. They can create annoyances and irritate our inner world. Non-serving energy cords are not healthy, physically, mentally, emotionally, and spiritually. It is worth saying again before we move on. Cords happen… They are not a conscious construction like a grounding cord. They are not being created purposefully for some insidious reason regardless of how they may be affecting us. But beware! Pay attention to your thoughts and emotions. It might be you who is creating the cords in the first place and not the other way around.

Energy vampires send one type of non-serving energy cords. Their cords often look like tentacles. Animals use tentacles for grasping, feeding, or sensing. Energy vampires use them to grasp onto your subtle energy field, knock you out of the present moment, and siphon your life force energy.

Energy cords can also disturb your inner world. They penetrate the auric field and can cause you to, based on the information transmitted, take responsibility for anything and everything. You might find yourself reacting to a situation because you are assuming that what you are experiencing in your inner world is yours and yours to deal with.

You may find yourself worrying, ruminating, or fixing things that were never your problem in the first place. This phenomenon is especially true if you are an empath and have people-pleasing tendencies. You sense their needs, wants, and desires, which can create a disturbance in your inner world. Then you are all too happy to do whatever it takes to eliminate the perceived discomfort.

This tendency is why narcissists fall in love with you. They are more than happy to dump "their stuff," spoken or unspoken, into your personal space. It is a winning situation for them, and you are more than willing to use your time and energy to resolve "it" for them. Isn't that what love is all about?

Energy cords can also interfere with your ability to gain closure and experience a sense of inner peace when trying to end a relationship. Your partner never projected the incredible energy and excitement you experienced early on in the relationship. You created it in your mind and from within your being.

All energy is neutral. We are just responding to the subtle vibrations sent to us. We chose to fill our one empty mental slot with happy thoughts early in a relationship. When the relationship ends, or is in turmoil, the neutral energy being transmitting to us, instead of being interpreted as fun and exciting, can instead trigger some of our deepest and darkest negative thoughts about the other person.

This is why, after months of separation, you might find yourself still getting upset by a memory from a past relationship. There might be remnant cords connecting the two of you, and they were recently thinking about you. You, in turn, received their communication, which activated a cycle of worry and rumination.

By now, you are probably wondering what you can do if you have unhealthy cords attached to you. Here are a couple of techniques you can use to rid yourself of these unwanted communication channels.

Epsom Salt Bath

Soaking in a bath with Epsom salts has a long history of helping to relax the body and clear it of negative energy. Add one-half to a full cup of Epsom salt into a hot bath and enjoy. Try adding some essential oils to the healing water. Lavender, lemon, peppermint, or frankincense, are traditionally used to remove negativity and uplift the spirit. Hold the intention, *"As I soak, any cords connected to me will be easily and effortlessly released and go down the bathtub drain."*

Pulling Cords Energy Cords

Cords can also be pulled out of your body as a way of eliminating them. Many energetic healers suggest cutting energy cords instead of pulling them out. Cord cutting, verses pulling, is an undesirable way of stopping communication from someone else. There is a violent feel to this act. It can send adverse shock waves down both ends of the cord.

Additionally, when you cut a cord, instead of pulling it, you leave a little bit of them inside of you. It is like cutting a weed at its base instead of pulling it out by its roots. The plant is less likely to grow back when it, and its roots, are removed.

The process used to pull cords is similar to deprogramming. Here, however, you will be focusing on removing energy cords. You might want to set up a chair across from you in the same way you did when you deprogrammed your body. This will support you and deepen your level of intention. Do not forget, cords can form when we project our thoughts, so if you find yourself worrying or ruminating about past events, you might want to check yourself for newly formed ones.

- *To utilize this method, begin by taking a nice deep breath and allowing your body to relax.*
- *Give yourself a new grounding cord.*
- *Take a moment to clean out your auric field.*
- *In your mind's eye, pretend you can see yourself sitting in the chair facing you.*
- *When you are ready, imagine you have a handful of your incredible magic purple dust.*
- *Toss the purple dust all over and around your mental image of yourself.*
- *Watch as the dust turns black when it rests on any energy cords connected to you.*
- *You might find one or two, or you might envision hundreds.*

- *They might center on one chakra or another, or you might find one in the middle of your back in one of your shoulders.*
- *Be open to anywhere they might appear.*
- *Reach out and grasp one of the newly exposed cords.*
- *You may sense this wire-like communication channel in your hand as you grasp it.*
- *Gently pull it out.*
- *Some cords penetrate just beneath the surface of the skin.*
- *Others may dig deep into your body, like a tree that has taken root into the depths of your being.*
- *Keep pulling on the cord until you see or sense the end of it coming out.*
- *Sometimes you might detect a slight "pop" as you successfully pull the tip of the cord out.*
- *Apply additional magic dust to check for deeper hidden cords and remove them as well.*
- *When you feel done or complete, take a few deep breaths.*
- *Allow your body to relax further as you enjoy the wonderful feeling of being alone in your body, mind, and psyche.*
- *Thank yourself, God, spirit, or the universe for your newfound freedom.*

Moving On

Hopefully, after ending your last unwholesome relationship, you afforded yourself with some time to put your house in order and did not jump right back into the dating scene. Without healing your inner wounds, at least some of them, you are guaranteed one thing – you will more than likely find yourself right back in another unhealthy relationship plagued by the same issues you had in the past or worse. You can pray things will be better, but if you do not work on yourself, you will never escape the unhealthy patterns you have been living your whole life.

Maybe you took a long hard look at your history, your core beliefs, your triggers, and your coping mechanisms and better understand how you tick and why. Maybe you took the time to find yourself, what you want, what you need, what you think, and what you feel. Maybe you decided to start loving yourself and valuing the extraordinary person that you are. Maybe you took the time to become mindful of your inner world, got in control of your chronic state of worry or rumination, and are creating new neural pathways filled with happiness and joy. Then, after all of this inner work, maybe you woke up one morning and decide it is time to move on.

Getting back on the relationship saddle, for many, can be a terrifying thing. The idea of opening ourselves up to being hurt again can be unbearable, and the thought of becoming trapped in another abusive relationship unthinkable. If you have spent any amount of time working on yourself, healing yourself, you are not stepping up to the table as the same person you entered your last relationship. Your efforts have provided you with tools, understanding, and insights that will help you avoid getting caught up in another damaging situation.

Now, this does not mean that you will never attract another narcissist. You are an empath. Your light shines brightly. You entice narcissists to you like a moth to a flame. The primary difference between a Wounded Healer and an unhealed empath is that a Wounded Healer will quickly extricate themselves from the situation and minimizing any upset or damage. They know who they are and what they want. They pay attention to their inner world and the insights spirit offers. They have learned how to love themselves and, more importantly, how to take appropriate action to support their self-care.

This process can take time. For some, it might be months, others years. Congratulate yourself on your massive decision to bring someone new into your life, regardless of how long it took.

This phase can be fun, intriguing, and exciting. It can also push every single one of your buttons and trigger some of your deepest fears and insecurities. You might see a narcissist around every corner and in every interaction you have. Red flags may fly. Some of what you are experiencing may be true, sometimes not so much.

If you grew up in a toxic household, you have probably never experienced what a healthy relationship looks or feels like. How can you tell, especially early on, if the person you are seeing is telling the truth? How do you know if they are really into you or if they are only love bombing and future faking you? How can you know if the bond you feel forming is real or if it is just part of their grandiose scheme?

You don't.

The only reliable way of discovering the truth about your new potential lover is to give it time. Time to get to know the person inside. Time to see if their actions match their words. Time to see if their mask starts to crack and fall off. Time to separate your fears and insecurities from the reality of what is going on. Time will also afford you the chance to decide if he or she is a good match for you.

Individuals, especially ones with deep self-esteem issues, will often find themselves getting involved with just about anyone who affords them some attention. Breathing is often their only criteria. They are willing to accept too much. They do not take their wants, needs, and desires into account. They do not choose. They often never decide if they like the person in the first place much less want to be with them. They were chosen. The mere fact that someone wanted them blinds them. Even if everything about the other person goes against their senses, sensibilities, and value systems, you might find them gleefully skipping down the hall chanting, "*He likes me. He likes me.*"

If you have spent any time address your issues and working to change who you are, it is essential to ask yourself a few silly little questions when meeting someone new. "*Do I like him or her?*" "*Do I want to spend time with them?*" "*Do I feel good on the inside when I am around them?*" If they have open sores on their backs, pick their nose, are a slob, or have ten screaming babies running around, you might find yourself falling in love with them regardless. If, on the other hand, your inner world is going "*ewwwwww*," then you might want to pay attention to that and be authentic to yourself.

Healing raises your vibration. The higher your vibration, the more luminous, the more filled with love and light you become. This state opens the door to bringing individuals into your life that resonate at your new higher frequency, oh, and narcissists. Nevertheless, you are strong enough and smart enough not to be fooled again. You are also willing, once discovered, to kick them to the curb. Bye-bye Debbie downer!

If the time has come and you are ready to bring a new romantic partner into your life, working with the Law of Attraction may help you find the man or woman of your dream, the real man or woman of your dreams, not some cheap imitation.

Working With The Law Of Attraction

All of creation, according to scholars, is made up of a number of universal laws. These laws, like gravity, permeate all that we see. They also control the fabric of the unobservable forces that make up our world. The Law of Attraction is one of these universal laws.

According to *Wikipedia*, the Law of Attraction is the belief that positive or negative thoughts bring positive or negative experiences into a person's life.

Many misconceptions surround how the Law of Attraction works. In recent days, proponents of the Law of Attraction have touted it as a way to manifest more money, better relationships, and increased opportunities in life. All you need to do, if you want a new car, is to think about the vehicle or hang up pictures of your ideal ride. They also recommend saying affirmations about how worthy you are or how much you deserve a brand new automobile. Some individuals even claim that if you purchase their book or their special widget, you can become rich and famous. Balderdash!

The basis for the Law of Attraction should not be focused on getting a new car, millions of dollars, fame, or fortunes, although it might happen. Its focus should be on keeping yourself in alignment with the flow of life. It is about keeping your life force energy moving. It is about being in your heart and not trapped in your mind. In this way, you can open yourself up and bring into reality those things that are for your highest good. The gross misunderstanding of how the Law of Attraction works explains why one person is successful, when tapping into it, and their counterpart falters.

Granted, the Law of Attraction does require a certain level of conscious direction. The vital part of working with it successfully centers on your thoughts and feelings. If you are feeling excited, enthusiastic, passionate, secure, happy, and joyful about a situation, you are sending out positive energy. Conversely, you are projecting negative energy if you are feeling anxious, stressed out, angry, resentful, or sad. These negative thoughts sabotage your ability to bring the good things you desire into your existence.

The universe, in turn, will respond enthusiastically, but neutrally, to both of these vibrations. It does not decide which is better for you; it just sends you back more of the same. Whatever you are thinking, such as about a car or increased abundance, is your request to the universe. If you are clear about what you want and see, feel, and experience it in your hearts, souls, and mind's eye, you can potentially bring into our reality. If you experience doubt, instead of attracting in what you want, many times, you end up manifesting the opposite. These failures only end up validating your worst nightmares. Intention, intention, intention... Positive intentions expand. Negative intentions contract.

There is always a caveat to everything in life. Here is the small print when talking about the Law of Attraction.

Sometimes our ego gets in the way and tries to request what it wants and not what is really for our best interest. The Law of Attraction follows the guidance of the soul, not the will and dictates of the mind or ego.

We all would like a trillion dollars, but we might have lessons to learn before we are ready to have the cold hard cash we think we deserve. If you are reading this book, you might want to be happy and feel content on the inside or desire to have a healthy and happy relationship with someone who cares. Your challenge, one you have already taken up, is how to shift your thoughts and emotions from lack and loss to ones of abundance. And, if a wonderful man or woman happens to cross your path as you stay in alignment with good positive thoughts, even better.

Part of succeeding, with the Law of Attraction, is paying attention to your intuition and the dictates of the soul. Discovering the desires of the soul, and not the ego, will ultimately help you get what you want. Letting the soul steer the path your life takes will also reduce the hurt, anxiety, frustration, and disappointment of a bruised ego.

The Law of Attraction is simple if you understand its basic premise. It is not about what you want, but at the same time, it is ALL about what you desire. It does not work when you come from a place of ego. It functions when your heart, mind, and soul are in alignment with your higher power – source. When aligned, miracles happen, and you can experience the life that you truly desire.

How To Work With The Law Of Attraction

There are four steps you should follow to maximize this process, be it finding a new job, a new car, or a new relationship. They are not hard and fast rules. Obsessing over one part or the other only interferes with the flow of your life force energy and your ability to manifest it onto the physical plane. The four steps are getting clear, commit yourself, taking action, and gratitude.

Getting Clear

First and primary on the list is you have to know what you want. You need a clear picture of it. By now, you should have a better understanding of who you are and what you want in your relationships. If you are unsure, perhaps making a list of all of the possibilities will help you narrow down your thought, ideas, and feelings.

For example, do you want your new potential mate to be neat, tidy, and well kept? Do they need to be financially independent? Do you want to be with someone kind, loving, and affectionate, attentive to you and your needs, articulate, and emotionally mature? Do you want them to hold your hand as you walk through the mall, snuggle with you in bed or smile lovingly at you across a crowded room?

These are only a few things you can contemplate as you identify your relationship needs. It is better to keep your requests general in nature. Putting a relationship with football quarterback Troy Aikman first and foremost on your list might be a bit much for the universe to muster up, so be realistic.

Also, try not to fill your list with negatives. Identifying the fact that you do not want to be with a slob will only work to defeat your purpose. The universe will not hear, "*I do not want to be with a slob*," but only "*slob.*" Rephrase your inventory from what you do not want to what you do. This list will also support you down the road once you start meeting people to help you weed out who you might want to keep from those you want to toss back.

Become mindful of any negative thought patterns that may arise as you do this. Remember, negative thinking only sabotages your ability to have what you truly desire. Breathe, ground, and ho'oponopono if need be. Trust that the universe has your best interests at heart. Trust dissolves fears. You cannot be afraid if you trust.

See it, feel it, experience it as if it were real. Imagine it in your mind's eye. Allow your desires to become emotionally charged. Believe in yourself and your future. Set your intentions. Feelings are the driving force behind the Law of Attraction. Our emotional energy activates our mental images and puts them in motion. They are then transmitted out into the universe via our chakras. Be patient while you await its reply.

Make A Commitment To Yourself

The next step to this equation is committing yourself. Recognize that there may be some time and effort required on your part or that you will have to take action. Ask yourself, *"what do I need to do to have this become a reality."* Sometimes it is as easy as picking up the phone and making a call. At other times, you may need to put a plan together about how you are going to bring your desires into reality. If the task seems overwhelming or unaccomplishable, break it down into smaller, more manageable chunks that are easier to achieve.

Napoleon Hill, in his book, *Think And Grow Rich*, identifies another reason why people fall short of experiencing their dreams. He believed that the most common cause of failure is quitting when we experience temporary defeat. Obstacles are often placed on our path to see how committed we are to the object of our desire. It can be likened to a test we must to take to ensure we have the right stuff. Just like in school, if you pass the test, you can move on to the next level.

Obstacles and failures may also be a sign that you are slightly off course. They can be used to help you refine, define, and clarify your objectives. Sometimes they help fine-tune you and get you to the perfect place, the ideal vibration inside. If you keep walking into a wall as you endeavor to move forward, many times, all it takes is a step to the left. This small act may allow you to begin moving forward again, effortlessly.

Taking Action

Taking action is a critical step in making your dreams come true. By taking even a small step toward achieving your goals, you will be setting the Natural Laws of the Universe into motion. Steps, regardless of their size, grease the gears of the universe and allow it to work in the way it is designed to function.

Many individuals believe all they need to do is create a vision board (a graphic representation, which can be used to help clarify your intentions), repeat affirmations, or maintain positive thoughts. Without action, nothing can be achieved. If you want a new relationship, hoping, wishing, and praying about it will do no good if you do not put yourself out there to meet new suitors.

Gratitude

The final piece, when working with the Law of Attraction, is gratitude. Say thank you for the blessings you receive. By recognizing and acknowledging even the smallest things you are receiving in your life, you can begin to open the door to receiving bigger and better things. Hopefully, that will culminate in the relationship you have been looking for your entire life.

Ultimately, the Law of Attraction is not about getting a new car, millions of dollars, fame, or fortunes. It is about keeping ourselves in alignment with the flow of life, allowing it and not our ego to lead the way. In this way, we open ourselves up to the grace of God and bring to ourselves those things we desire. And to this and all that we receive - thank you.

Internet What?

As you read the last section on the Law of Attraction, you were probably asking yourself, "*Where can I meet Mr. or Mrs. Right?*" Meeting new people, especially if you are over 40, can be challenging. The internet does provide a viable solution – internet dating.

"*Why would I want to do that?*" Or "*Do I seem that desperate that I have go online to find someone?*" are common kneejerk reactions to this suggestion. You could always try the bar scene, start going to church, or become more involved with community events to expand your horizon of unattached singles. You could hope that some stranger would ask for your phone number at the supermarket or a concert or trade show, but the chances of that happening seem unlikely. Anyway, would you, in reality, want to provide someone you have just met your personal information?

There are many great reasons to try online dating. First off, you can do it from the comfort of your own home. Next, there is anonymity. You do not have to give out your name, your location, or any personal information. (We will talk more about this and other online dating safety points a little later on).

Online dating allows you to get to know a person and create rapport before you ever setting eyes on them. It is a great way to meet members of the opposite sex (or same-sex) if you are bashful or gun-shy about getting involved with someone new. It lets you try a relationship on for size and see how it fits. If it does not work for you, you can move on. And, bad as this is to say aloud, nothing feels better than having your ego stroked by someone who may be interested in you.

If you decide to give online dating a spin, here are a few pointers to begin. We have all seen commercials for sites like Match.com or E-Harmony.com, but they are not the only fish in the preverbal dating sea. There are a large number of websites you can choose from, some free, others are fee-based. Each site has its own tone and timbre. Look around the site to see if what they offer appeals to you.

Before signing up for any dating sites, for safety's sake, create a separate yahoo or Gmail email account. This simple act will further protect your anonymity while providing you with an email address you can use for future correspondence.

You will be asked to create a personal profile to give people an idea of who you are. Only provide information you feel comfortable exposing to the general public. Remember, anyone on the site can read what you have posted. Be perky and upbeat as you describe yourself. Talk about what you want. Post the positive, not the negative. There is nothing wrong with identifying a deal-buster, but if all you talk about is what you do not want, you might turn someone good away.

All sites will also ask you to upload a photo of yourself. Please, please, please, use a real picture. There is nothing worse than meeting someone only to find out they used a Victoria's Secret or Chippendales picture on the site to represent themselves. Just as bad, is posting a picture of yourself that is twenty or thirty years old. It does not represent who you are. If down the road, you do choose to meet that special someone you have been taking to online, there is nothing worse than the look of surprise or perhaps disappointment on their face when they see you for the first time.

Once you have your information up online, explore the site. Search for individuals in your area. Read their profiles. Have fun. Talk to the people who contact you if you are so inclined. Reach out and contact people who seem interesting. They do not know who you are, so enjoy just being you.

One thing you will quickly find out is that not all dating sites are the same. On one website, you might get inundated with "hits" from interested parties. On another, you might not get any or only a few. Some sites might have a lot of members, but not many in your geographical area. On others, the majority of people you encounter, might seem creepy, offensive, or want more than you are willing to give. There are even dating sites devoted to connecting people for casual sex (hook-ups). Go for it, if that is all you want.

With that said, pick and chose. Feel free to post your information on multiple sites until you find one that feels right. As they say, location, location, location.

One of the great things about this type of dating is that if someone writes to you and your skin curls, you do not have to respond. In the same way, if they start off nice and the conversation quickly changes direction leaving you feeling uncomfortable, such as they ask for money or profess their undying love for you within the first few messages, you can quickly cut off contact. Many dating sites give you the option to block someone from communicating with you, thus eliminating any problems you may encounter.

Things are going good. You are enjoying your conversations with your new friend. Then what? The trend today is to exchange phone numbers and text quickly. How any of this moves forward is all up to you. You can pace it however fast or however slow you want or need it to be. You can give out your number or not. If the person you are talking to does not like the pace you have set, oh well, move on. They were probably not right for you in the first place.

Here are a few safety tips when talking about phones. Some people purchase disposable cell phones they use solely for dating. By using the disposable telephone, you are not giving out your home or primary cell phone number. This additional step will keep a bit of distance between you and the now not so strange stranger. It will give you time to decide if you feel comfortable enough with them and want to let them further in your life and your business.

So far, so good. Things are going well, and you are ready for your first big meeting. To ensure your safety, here are some other safety tips you should consider. Probably the most crucial piece of advice is to meet initially in a public place. Never have them pick you up at home, thus disclosing where you live. Drive your car to the rendezvous. If you feel uncomfortable or if things do not go as planned, you can always leave.

Starbucks is always a great place to have a first encounter for a number of reasons. One, there are millions of them all around the country. Two, a latte costs around $5.00. Three, if you are not having fun, a $5.00 drink will not leave you feeling obligated to stay or pay in more ways than one.

It is also a good idea to make sure a friend or a family member knows where you are going and what you are planning. If you change your plans, always let someone know. Some people will have a friend call them shortly after the commencement of a meeting. This call does two things. It lets your friend know you are safe and sound. Sadly, you could use that same phone call as an excuse to cut the date short and exit quickly stage left.

If you find yourself becoming involved with someone who lives far away, and decide to meet in person, here are a few things to consider. Rent a car at the airport if you fly. Make your hotel reservation yourself, whether you fly or drive, and keep its location to yourself. Once you are in town, meet in a public place, as described earlier. If the meeting does not go well, the privacy you afforded yourself can provide you with a safe haven.

Hopefully, your first date will turn into one of many, and you will live the rest of your life happily with your newfound lover. If that is not the case, it is not the end of the world. As they say, some will, some won't, move on.

Using an online dating site is not dating itself. It is, nevertheless, a great way to connect with others. It can give you the freedom and flexibility to be who you are and the chance to get to know someone before you ever meet. So if you are looking for a special someone, give online dating a try. You will have nothing to lose.

Then What...

Thankfully, we can all fall in love again. As our heart melts, releasing our past trauma, we can begin to love ourselves and hopefully experience true love with a terrific partner. How your next relationship develops and what it will look like is hard to predict, but here are some insights into how a healthy relationship should be.

We feel safe when we are in a loving relationship. We feel secure enough to open our hearts and minds to another. Our internal feelings of safety afford us the possibility of expressing ourselves and our inner world without fear of repercussion. Relationships, regardless of the kind, are all about give and take. An ideal dynamic is often characterized as being 50 – 50, with both parties being willing to commit their time and energy into making the relationship work.

The early stages of a new romantic relationship are easy. You meet. Everything is fresh, exciting, and new. It is easy for you to put a great deal of yourself into the relationship. As you learn more about your significant other, you enjoy the deepening feelings and increased closeness. This is one of the best parts of falling in love.

This dynamic does shift over time. The fast-paced excitement of the initial stages of a relationship will start to slow down. You may feel like the forward movement that you initially experienced has stopped and may wonder if you are "falling out of love." These feelings are a normal part of the process.

As the initial drive starts to fade, instead of devoting your attention to your relationship, other things may begin to claim your time and energy. Instead of it being easy, you now have to make a conscious choice to contribute. If you are involved with a narcissist, this is where your relationship will begin to fail. The change in your attention away from them to other matters is what causes a narcissist's mask to crumble and their true colors to emerge.

Our partners need two things from us – our time and our attention. Of the two, our attention is more important.

Without paying attention to their wants, needs, and desires, we are inadvertently saying to them that they are low on our totem pole and not valued in our eyes.

According to Jason Ivers, in his article, *The Truth Behind Falling – And Being – In Love*, "*Giving time without attention is sort of like leaving a seventeen cent tip at a restaurant... it lets the other person know that you didn't forget, you just didn't think they were worthy of more. It's insulting, whether done consciously, as with the tip, or subconsciously, as with spending time with your significant other without giving them your full attention.*"

For wounded empaths and individuals who are people pleasers, taking your partner's wants and needs into account is probably not your issue. You may have become very used to the dynamic between the two of you feeling more like 70 – 30 or 80 – 20, with you putting in the 70 or 80% and them the remainder. This dynamic is not anywhere close to the idealized 50 – 50. For individuals like you, the more significant challenge is not about giving more. It is about setting limits to your giving. The operative word here is "boundaries."

Boundaries: The Foul 10 Letter Word

Boundaries are kind of like cords. We only ever need to have them when we are interacting with other people. They are the last stop on our journey and are the final piece required for you to find and be your authentic self.

Boundaries define limits. They are like a border that demarks where we end, and another begins. Boundaries help us be clear about who we are and afford us the prospect of expressing what we think and how we feel. They allow us to establish our line in the sand, where we can ensure that others treat us with honor, dignity, and respect as well as letting them know when they are acting in inappropriate or in unacceptable ways.

Boundaries are sometimes described as being like a wall around us. The wall may be high, thick, and built of impenetrable stones, or it may be low, weak, and easily breached by anyone. The first type ensures that no one can ever hurt us. It keeps us safe but isolated from intimacy and support. The second kind leaves us vulnerable to abuse and manipulation. In the end, neither style boundary serves us well.

In relationships where our level of involvement and risk is low, such as with the people we work with or the salesperson at the store, it is relatively easy to exert our boundaries. It is in our intimate relationships, ones with close friends, romantic partners, and our families that they can be challenging to maintain. Children who grew up in a traumatic household often find that they have very weak or no boundaries at all. They may have had their boundaries violated so often they may not even recognize when it happens.

How can you tell if one of your boundaries has been violated? You will detect disturbances in your inner world.

Individuals may find themselves exploited by people who are controlling or who possess narcissistic tendencies if they are people-pleasers, who cannot express themselves and create and maintain healthy boundaries. If this is you, you may find yourself dwelling on what you want or need in a situation but are too afraid to share it. The abuser will quickly see that you have a hard time being assertive and voicing your opinion, have a weak sense of self, and exhibit a willingness to suffer at the their expense. These unwholesome individuals, if given a chance, will take as much as they can from you and give nothing in return.

If you, by now, have discovered that you have a hard time expressing your inner world, recognize the only way you will ever be authentic to yourself is to put your big girl panties on and reveal your truth. It can take every bit of courage you can muster to have the words you have been sequestering inside leave your lips. If you find yourself bracing for impact or cringing in anticipation of an unfavorable reaction, do not blame yourself. You developed this reaction as a child. It is part of your dysfunctional programming.

It is only by taking positive actions to correct what is eating away at you that you can find that happy place inside. Is it hard? Heck yeah, it is hard, especially if you have never done it before.

Being open to sharing what you think and what you feel can be extremely scary, but it is also a very loving act. You are loving yourself. It lets the world know that you honor and respect yourself and are willing to do what it takes to care for you. For many, this is huge, huge!

Creating boundaries and requesting that our needs be met may feel harsh, rude, and demanding. However, Sherry Pagoto Ph.D., in her article, *Are you a People Pleaser?* informs us, "*We teach people how to treat us by the behavior we accept or reject from them. If someone takes advantage of you, it is only their fault once. After that it is your fault for not teaching them different. Teaching different means setting boundaries about what you can and cannot do, and what you will and will not accept.*"

Oh, and in case you were wondering, having boundaries will not make you a narcissist either. Just sayin'.

Before I Go

Thank you for sharing my journey, our journey, from dysfunction to living a healthier and fuller life as a Wounded Healer. With the insights, tools, and tips you have gleaned from this text, you should be able to begin moving forward, experiencing life in a more wholesome way.

Understanding your upbringing, your inner wounding, and the patterns and cycles expressed by your inner world may have helped you to figure out how you got into this situation in the first place. By knowing the telltale signs of narcissism and narcissistic abuse, you now have the awareness required to recognize when it is safe to stay and when you need to go.

Lastly, you have begun the process of reducing the effects of negative, intrusive thoughts your inner wounding triggers. You have also started creating new neural pathways geared towards peace, happiness, and living a life in the present moment. Combined, you are actively transforming your life from experiencing repeated patterns of toxic relationships into finding your true authentic self and someone to share it with. Congratulate yourself on all you have accomplished.

Before I say goodbye, I want to give you an update on my journey.

I have loved two men in my life. Better said, I have had two men love me for who I am. They loved me with my bad hair and sarcastic humor. They saw beneath the surface of my sexuality and what I could offer them. They accepted me unconditionally with all of my flaws and foibles. I lost one to cancer and the other one I am going to tell you about now.

I have included this update to share some unexpected emotional events that would never have transpired had I not met him. He has been a blessing and at the same time, has elicited intense emotions that would never have come to the surface without him in my life. Regardless of how much work we do on ourselves, it is not until we are in a relationship that life events can and will create circumstances that will activate more entrenched wounding. These situations afford us additional opportunities to heal.

It had been about four months since I had gotten rid of my last narcissistic boyfriend. He is the person I talked about at the beginning of this book. I was not planning on or even hoping to meet someone new but decided to go online and check it out. Was I ready, hell no! I thought dating, just dating, would allow me the chance to use my new relationship tools.

I wanted to test my ability to establish boundaries. I wanted to observe my inner world in my dealings, deciding what was working and what was not. I was committed to listening to myself and what my body was telling me and act as my own advocate. I knew I had to love myself and respect myself regardless of any relationship cost. I was going to choose and not be chosen.

I decided to join Match.com and had only been online for about a month. I was talking to several people when I received a message from Razorback. He had a weird profile picture but also had a picture of him jumping out of an airplane in full military gear. That was intriguing. We started talking, and I was immediately impressed. He was smart and seemed sincere. And for whatever reason, things moved forward quickly.

In short order, we had exchanged email addresses. One of the first emails I received was Razorback's full bio. It seemed like he was telling me everything about his life, his career, and his failed marriages. It was much more than I would have expected so early on. It was honest and open - refreshing. I decided to respond in kind and told him about my life, my work, and my multiple failed marriages. If he was not holding back, why should I?

It was only a few weeks after our initial correspondence that I was booked to appear at a metaphysical conference close to his home, so I asked him if he wanted to meet for dinner. That was a first for me. I have never asked a guy out on a first date. Well, the big day came, and I happened to be standing outside when a big red truck rolled past. Oh my God, it was him.

I was giddy like a schoolgirl. I had butterflies in my stomach, and when he walked up to me in his jacket and tie, I thought I was either going to die or that my beet-red face would give me away. I was so out of it that I sent a girlfriend a couple of texts telling her that I was a mess and how cute he was, only to find out at the end of the evening, I had accidentally sent the texts to him. OOPS?

Things kept moving forward. By the end of our second weekend together, I looked him in the face and told him that I could fall in love with him. Then I started crying. I am not a crier and have never bawled in front of another person. He asked me what was wrong and what exploded from my lips was, "*don't hurt me.*" Then I lost it and wept in his arms. That was another first.

I was so scared and felt extremely vulnerable, which was another new experience for me. What if I opened my heart to him and he turned out to be another narcissist? He seemed to be kind, loving, and straightforward, but this could have just been his way of love bombing me. Was there a mean and nasty person hiding behind a mask of compassion? I did not know. What I did know was that the only way to discover the truth was to give it a chance. It could be really, really great or it could suck big-time. I knew I was ready. I knew what to look for, and was prepared to analyze all of his actions waiting for the other shoe to drop, hoping and praying it would not.

It was amazing and terrifying all at the same time.

So this is where things stood by the end of the first month. The job Razorback had been working had recently ended. He lived, in his precise words, 148.2 miles away in an RV. Since he had retired from the Army Rangers as a Lieutenant Colonel, he did not need to work and thought he could move closer to me and help around my big old house.

Red alert! Red alert! Danger, Will Robinson, danger! Can you add future faking to that order of love bombing? To say I panicked was an understatement.

I was not ready for that, but I could also understand his concern about not wanting to drive the long distance regularly. I knew I did not want him to go away, and though all of my internal warnings were going off, I gave him the green light to move closer. Could I trust him? Was this just a ploy? The verdict was pending.

I was all over the place and an emotional mess. I would be happy one day and crying and raw the next. I would break down weeping because he was kind to me. Then I would cry even more because I felt so damaged. The mere thought of getting so upset because someone was nice to me left me in hysterics. But, as I would be going through one of my many emotional meltdowns, he would hold me in his nurturing arms and tell me, *"If this is the worst you've got, this ain't shit."* He would then reassure me that he was not going anywhere. That would only make me cry more. I do not know why he stayed, but he did.

I think it is hard for someone who had a healthy upbringing to understand the impact long-termed abuse has on our psyches. You cannot just let it go. It is a part of you, deeply embedded in your soul. With this new relationship, I was even more committed to working on myself and moving through my negative core beliefs and other harmful programs that had formed over the years.

Is my journey done? No. There is still more to work on, but by the end of three months, lots of crying, lots of looking and observing myself and my triggers, I let him move in with me. I have come to trust him implicitly, well unless I am triggered, that is, but I am a work in progress. He is my friend, my partner, my confidant. I love him deeply, and as I have said over and over throughout this book, your dreams can come true. I know mine have.

About Rita Louise, PhD

A gifted and talented clairvoyant medical intuitive, Dr. Rita Louise helps people identify the root causes of their concerns. She is a Naturopathic physician and the founder of the Institute Of Applied Energetics that trains students in the art of medical intuition, intuitive counseling, and energy medicine. She is the author of the books *Stepping Out Of Eden, ET Chronicles: What Myth And Legend Have To Say About Human Origin, Avoiding The Cosmic 2X4, Dark Angels: An Insider's Guide To Ghosts, Spirits & Attached Entities* and *The Power Within*.

She is also the producer of a number of feature length as well as video shorts. Their titles include: *iKon: Deconstructing The Archetypes Of The Ancients, Holy Deception, Ancient Aliens, Genetic Engineering & The Rise Of Civilization, The Truth About The Nephilim Giants, Deceit, Lies & Deception: The Reptilian Agenda, Paranormal Phenomena: Attached Entities – The Bad Kids Of The Spirit World, Ghosts, Gods & Myth, The Secret To The Law Of Attraction* and *Reincarnation: Have We Been Here Before*?

Dr. Louise credits early childhood influences for the direction her life would take. By the age of 8, she developed a deep interest in ancient traditions, culture, archaeology and human origins. As time went on, she began searching for spiritual self-discovery pursuing topics including health and wellness, philosophy and the esoteric arts and sciences. Dr. Louise graduated San Jose State University with a degree in Industrial Design and worked as an electro-mechanical designer and Engineering Services Manager in the *military* industrial complex. She is a graduate of the Berkeley Psychic Institute where she studied meditation, energy medicine, and learned how to perform clairvoyant readings. After establishing a private practice, Dr. Louise returned to school full time, earning a degree as a Naturopath and then a Ph.D. in Natural Health Counseling.

A frequent consultant to the media, Dr. Louise has appeared on television and film and has mystified listeners during her countless radio interviews. Dr. Louise has appeared as a keynote speaker at hundreds of events around the country where she has spoken on topics such as ancient mysteries, mythology, ancient aliens, intuition, ghosts and the paranormal. Her countless writings have appeared in books, magazines and newsletters around the world.

Her webpage is SoulHealer.com.

Stepping Out Of Eden

Does our genetic make-up determine our humanity? Is it our biological differences, our lack of body hair, the size of our brains, opposable thumbs or our ability to walk upright? While countless hours are spent investigating our biology, little time is invested in figuring out why we do the things we do, think the way we think and experience the world in the way we have.

Stepping Out Of Eden takes the concept of human origin to a whole new level. In its exploration of this ancient mystery, it delves into our foundational beliefs, thoughts, actions, and deeds. It asks the question why do humans act human? What caused us to transition from ape to man? Did we evolve, as contemporary science says, or did a group of extraterrestrial visitors mold us into who we are today?

Stepping Out Of Eden combines information from theological sources and the mythic record with archeological finds to create a broad view of who we are and where the essence of humanity comes from.

This book is long overdue. It blends both sides of human endeavor both with style, insight, and clarity. It is pieced together in a cohesive narrative that leads on to a final question "Who Are We". This book is without equal and long overdue.
– Steven Strong and Evan Strong

The E.T. Chronicles: What Myths and Legends Tell Us About Human Origins

The E.T. Chronicles is a startling and comprehensive examination of ancient myths and legends that describe extraterrestrial visitors and their encounters with humanity since the dawn of time. Organized into a chronology that starts with *"in the beginning"* and ends with the advent of civilization, it brings together myths from many cultures (including the Sumerians, the Greek, the Maya and the Aborigines of Australia) and explores them in the context of current scientific discoveries.

The result is a mind-blowing re-visioning of human origins through close reading of ancient texts relating to: creation, gods and goddesses, heaven, the gods and their toys (space ships or chariots?), the quest for immortality

Could it be that those ancient stories of the gods were more than just the product of someone's fanciful imagination? Is it possible that the writers, chroniclers, and scribes of our distant past actually record an accurate view of our origin? Could it be that we are really children of the stars?

> "Absolutely fascinating and a must read for anyone interested in the 'extraterrestrial question' of the origins of humanity."
> Robert M. Schoch, Ph.D.

Dark Angels: An Insider's Guide To Ghosts, Spirits & Attached Entities

When talking about beings without bodies; angels, ascended masters and spirit guides aren't the only kids on the block. Dark Angels talks about the bad kids in town. Who are these bad kids? As a child, you might have met one at night…under your bed, in your closet or down a dark hallway. What are we talking about? We are talking about ghosts, spirits and attached entities.

Dark Angels is an exciting exploration into the darker side of the spirit world. This isn't a dull dissertation about ghosts. It takes a fun and candid approach to addressing ghosts, attached entities and demons. Dark Angels is filled with revealing information about these "*dark forces*" and how they can influence our lives.

Written in a straightforward, easy to read manner, the technical content as well as the stories shared are infused with Dr. Louise's own wit, candor and sassy style.

Dr. Rita Louise has done it again with her new book
Dark Angels!
Wayne L. – Dallas, TX

Films by Rita Louise, PhD

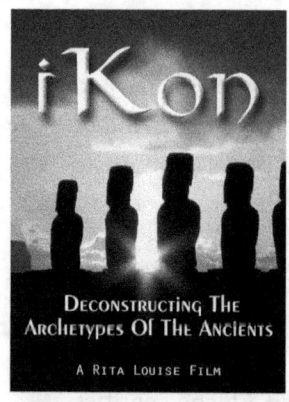

iKon: Deconstructing the Archetypes of the Ancients

iKon: Deconstructing The Archetypes of the Ancients challenges you to open your mind to a completely new way of thinking of our past, a past that is being hidden from us, yet is right in front of our very eyes. Are you ready to step outside the box of conventional thought?

Holy Deception

What do you believe about God? Holy Deception challenges you to reexamine your notion of God while looking at what other cultures, both past and present have to say. Is our current perception of God actually a flight of fantasy? Could we have been deceived and our notion of a kind and benevolent omnipotent creator god be fallacious? Dr. Rita Louise's new film is a mix of Ancient Aliens VS. the Bible!

Available on Amazon.com

www.ingramcontent.com/pod-product-compliance
Lightning Source LLC
Chambersburg PA
CBHW050618300426
44112CB00012B/1558